THE SOCIAL SECURITY

PROGRAM

in the

UNITED STATES

by

CHARLES I. SCHOTTLAND

Appleton-Century-Crofts

Division of Meredith Publishing Company

New York

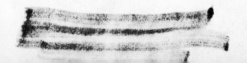

PREFACE

Social security programs in the United States have grown so rapidly that in spite of the numerous publications relating to social security programs, there is still a lack of knowledge on the part of many about their essential features.

This book, therefore, has been written primarily for the person interested in obtaining a brief overview of the social security program. It is not intended to be an analysis of the many issues around social security measures.

I wish to acknowledge the helpfulness of many friends and associates who reviewed and commented on the final manuscript. I am particularly grateful to Robert J. Myers, Chief Actuary of the Social Security Administration, United States Department of Health, Education, and Welfare, for reviewing a substantial number of the chapters, particularly those relating to old-age, survivors, and disability insurance; to Charles E. Hawkins, Legislative Reference Officer in the Office of the Commissioner of the Social Security Administration, for his review of the chapter on public assistance; to Roger Cumming, Director of Social Work Services, Veterans Administration, for his review of the chapter relating to veterans' benefits; to Robert M. Ball, Commissioner of Social Security, who reviewed an early draft; to members of the staff of the Social Security Administration, who reviewed the material in several chapters, and particularly to Elizabeth G. Sanders and other staff of the Division of Program Analysis of the Social Security Administration, who commented on many of the chapters; to Robert C. Goodwin, Director of the Bureau of Employment Security, United States Department of Labor, who reviewed the chapter on Unemployment Insurance; to Andrew R. N. Truelson, Assistant Director of the Bureau of Family Services of the Welfare Administration of the Department of Health, Education, and Welfare, and staff of the Bureau who reviewed the chapters on Public Assistance and General Assistance; and, finally, to my wife, Edna L. Schottland, who typed the first draft of the manuscript and encouraged me to undertake the book in the first place.

CHARLES I. SCHOTTLAND

v

CONTENTS

FOREWORD BY
LORD BEVERIDGE

I am glad that this book has been written and will be published almost at once. I am delighted to have been given the chance of knowing the ground covered by all the chapters of this book and of reading the Introduction with special care. For this Introduction makes clear two points of great importance.

The first point is that government action to bring social security to the citizen did not begin with the making of the Beveridge Report in 1942. In Britain, it began, as I have often said, before World War I, and the idea of giving a free health service is over six hundred years old, having been applied in Westminster in 1300. In the United States, as Mr. Schottland's book shows, it was largely a reaction to the Great Depression of 1933, between World Wars I and II.

The second point is that the social security systems of different countries are very different in themselves, in the ground they cover, the methods by which they are financed, and the conditions on which help is given by the State to the citizen.

The Beveridge Report, for all the acclamation it received, has in some respects not been carried out, particularly in regard to old people. There appears at present to be some risk of growing departure from its central principles. The Beveridge Report was not designed to bring into being a Welfare State in which the citizen would get everything he could possibly want in the way of welfare from the State without making any contribution of his own or taking thought for himself. Its central principle is welfare by co-operation between the State and the citizen, the State guaranteeing the citizen against actual want in any of the unavoidable misfortunes of life, while leaving to the citizen freedom and responsibility for the management of his affairs and those of his dependents above the basis of security established by the State.

The essential condition of freedom and responsibility for the citizen is avoidance by the State of any form of means test in dealing with the citizens. If the State, before giving any help to a citizen, asks whether he has any resources of his own, that is equivalent to telling him not to think for himself. "If you have saved nothing for yourself or your children, I will give you everything that you or they need; if you have thought and saved for yourself, I will give you less."

The people of the United States, by strong tradition, stand for independence and responsibility of the citizen, for everything in his power. If, while extending State action for things that the State alone can do in social security, they keep to this tradition, they will become the natural leaders of humanity in this field.

Mr. Schottland has set the facts of the United States program fairly before us all. His book should have many readers and lead the world to still more welfare with freedom and independence and responsibility for the citizen.

25 October 1962

TABLES IN TEXT

Tables in Appendix

THE SOCIAL SECURITY PROGRAM
IN THE UNITED STATES

"The era of freedom will be achieved only as social security and human welfare become the main concern of men and nations." [1] —*W. L. MacKenzie King*

CHAPTER I

INTRODUCTION

The comment on the preceding page by the eminent Canadian statesman, W. L. MacKenzie King, is indicative of the world-wide recognition of the importance of social security programs in the modern world.

Along with other nations, the United States has taken note that "An attempt to find security for a people is among the oldest of political obligations and the greatest task of the state."[2] The social security system in the United States is relatively young as compared with such systems in European countries. Yet its growth has been phenomenal, its impact on the American economy significant, and its place as an American institution firmly established.

To promote security, and particularly economic security, all of the industrial nations of the world have developed a variety of social security programs. Some have taken the form of "social insurance" whereby contributions are made to a fund by workers, employers, self-employed persons, and governments, and payments are made to persons whose income has stopped for such reasons as old age, disability, unemployment, or death of the wage earner. Other programs have taken the form of "social assistance" whereby persons in need receive public relief or pensions by virtue of age or for other reasons. Still other social assistance programs have taken the form of "social benefits" whereby all persons meeting certain qualifications such as attainment of a prescribed age and having a certain period of citizenship or residence receive benefits, without regard to any previous contributions or taxes paid or demonstration of individual need.

Whatever method has been adopted, the primary aim has been to replace income lost because of broad social and economic factors,

1

or to provide a minimum floor of protection through the maintenance of a minimum cash income.

These measures adopted by various nations have increasingly been called "Social Security."

The term "Social Security" first appeared prominently in the United States Social Security Act.[3] Its use spread rapidly throughout the world and the mention of social security in the Atlantic Charter of 1941 gave it further impetus.[4]

In some countries the term "Social Security" covers all governmental programs aimed at achieving the maintenance of income; in others it applies primarily to social insurance; in others it covers a variety of health and welfare services. Even within the United States the term is used in a number of ways. Although most persons identify social security with old-age, survivors, and disability insurance, "social security" in the United States covers a variety of programs including social insurance programs providing cash benefits for unemployment (unemployment insurance), cash benefits in old age, for disability or death (old-age, survivors, and disability insurance), cash payments to persons in need (public assistance or relief), and a variety of health and welfare services under the Social Security Act.

Since the major programs of social security involve some type of cash payment to assure at least a minimum income, this book will describe briefly the history and background of the "income maintenance" programs of social security in the United States.

These programs are large and significant. In 1962, the sums paid out in benefits under these various social security programs constituted an annual expenditure which exceeded the total national budgets of many of the large countries of the world.

In spite of the rapid growth of the United States social security programs, however, they are not well understood either in the United States or abroad. In the fall of 1957, the Executive Committee of the International Social Security Association (ISSA) met in Rome. This governing board was composed of the top officials of social security programs in nineteen countries.

In the discussion which ensued, the representatives expressed amazement at the rapid growth of social security programs in the United States. The attitude of these officials was expressed by one of the Italian delegates when he said, "For more than fifty years, we in Europe have assumed that democratic goals must include the replacement of earnings lost through factors outside the control of the individual such as old age, unemployment, death of the wage earner, or sickness. On the other hand, the traditional image we have had of the United States is that the worker is well-off when working, but the state has little interest in him when he is unemployed or too old to work. Today even some Italians living in Italy are receiving social security benefits from the United States and we are obliged to change the image we have of the American system when more than twenty million persons are receiving some form of social security under it."

In subsequent travels through France, Germany, Switzerland, Austria, and the Soviet Union as well as in conversation with numerous foreign officials from countries all over the world, it became evident to the writer that social security programs in the United States were not well understood, even by officials engaged in the administration of social security programs in other countries.

In questioning many people, including some political and business representatives in leadership roles in this country, it became obvious that social security in the United States, although now firmly established, is not well understood even by many in the United States. Yet the desire on the part of the public to learn about the rights, benefits, and obligations of individuals under the program is so pressing that almost seventy-five newspapers run daily question-and-answer columns on social security; during the past year, at least fifty important nationally distributed periodicals have published articles on the subject; and the pamphlet "Your Social Security" [5] published by the Social Security Administration is one of the most popular of government pamphlets and millions of copies have been distributed.

This book will present a brief and simple summary of social security programs in the United States. It will not discuss these in detail, nor will it attempt to examine, except briefly, the many significant issues involved in the growth, development, and future status of social security and related programs.

In 1962, social insurance, public assistance, and related social security programs paid benefits to about thirty million persons, through a number of programs, as indicated below in Figure 1.

Figure 1

Social Security and Public Income Maintenance Monthly Payments and Beneficiaries for Month of April 1962 (in millions)

	Beneficiaries	Payments
Old-Age, Survivors, and Disability Insurance	17.0	$1,201.0
Public Assistance	7.5	375.0
Unemployment Insurance, temporary disability, and workmen's compensation	2.5*	643.0
Railroad and Federal Civil Service employee retirement	1.4	167.0
Veterans' compensation and pensions	4.7	308.0
Total April 1962 payments (in millions)	33.1†	$2,694.0

* Average weekly for unemployment insurance only.

† This is the total of above figures and includes a certain amount of duplication of persons receiving benefits under more than one program. The unduplicated total is estimated at about thirty million persons.

Note: The above data do not include certain Federal employee retirement systems such as military retirement (about $75 million per month in benefits), and state and local retirement systems (about $100 million per month in benefits).

During the same year, benefits were being paid to beneficiaries all over the world—110,000 of them living abroad—persons who had earned these benefits through work covered by the Social Security Act or who were dependents of such workers.

Just as the social security systems of other countries were the results of each country's unique historical development, the American social security system was influenced by factors indigenous to the United States. The western frontier, the emphasis on self-help and voluntary programs, local self-government, states' rights—these and many other factors—political, economic, demographic, social, and philosophical, have influenced its development.

The rise of social insurance programs in Europe in the latter part of the nineteenth and beginning of the twentieth centuries had little impact on the United States. The American frontier, ever expanding, provided the possibility of economic security to anyone willing to leave the developed cities of the eastern United States. Every man could earn a living on land available from the government, either free or at a nominal cost. An Act of Congress in 1800 which cut the price of western public lands to $2 an acre was, in a sense, America's first social security program. Undoubtedly, this resource of land for the asking delayed the pressures and necessity for many types of social insurance. In addition, the rising standard of living of the American people during the period of industrialization delayed consideration of "security" measures.

The growth of voluntary insurance has likewise slowed the development of any comprehensive form of health insurance. In contradistinction to European countries, where voluntary health insurance covers only a small fraction of the population, in 1962 130 million persons (out of a population of 180 million), or two-thirds of the population, had some form of health insurance. Although such voluntary coverage is inadequate in many respects, covering for the most part only hospital bills (in some cases only partially), it has cushioned the economic impact of illness and has resulted in less pressure for a governmental health insurance program. The emphasis on voluntaryism and states' rights has also kept workmen's compensation (the program providing protection against the risk of industrial injuries and diseases) a state program with most employers insuring their workers through private insurance under the requirements of a state law.

Political factors likewise have shaped the United States program. The emphasis on states' rights has resulted in certain programs such as unemployment insurance and public assistance being administered by the individual states.

In none of the specific social security risks does government carry sole responsibility. Individual action and organized private action intermingle with and supplement government action in every field. Thus, old-age insurance under the Social Security Act is supplemented for millions of industrial and commercial workers by retirement and pension plans of industries and labor unions; survivors' insurance benefits under the Social Security Act are supplemented by a variety of public and private programs, including group life insurance provided by many employers and individual life insurance carried by the vast majority of America's gainfully employed.

These and other factors have resulted in a United States program which has responded piecemeal to a variety of economic risks, which has presented the least challenge to the voluntary principle and to voluntary insurance, which has maintained a large measure of state participation, and which therefore still has many gaps.

Nevertheless, in many respects it is a more comprehensive and co-ordinated system than most other countries have. Coverage under the old-age, survivors, and disability insurance (OASDI) program includes almost all self-employed persons and most agricultural and domestic workers—groups frequently excluded from coverage in many of the older systems—and the administration of the program is more closely integrated than in some foreign systems.

"Needs that were narrow or parochial a century ago may be interwoven in our day with the well-being of the nation. What is critical or urgent changes with the times." [6] —*Helvering v. Davis*

CHAPTER II

BACKGROUNDS

Throughout history, man has been concerned with his economic security and has devised various measures to cope with this problem. The huge granary reserves built by Joseph in Egypt were an attempt to make life more secure by storing food during years of plenty and distributing food during years of scarcity. The extended families in primitive societies were also a method of "spreading the risk" in that a large number of persons would have collective responsibility for the well-being of all of its members. This responsibility was later assumed by the tribe or other social unit.

Organized methods of providing some measure of economic security took very simple forms in primitive societies. Food storage, following the seasons, and migration as practiced by nomadic peoples—these and other simple measures were society's answer to the problem of securing the basic necessities of life. Although these primitive methods were frequently ineffective, they did serve to alleviate some hardships in an agrarian and uncomplicated society. Furthermore, the prevailing belief until the nineteenth century, which considered poverty to be the result of improvidence, vice, and laziness, mitigated against man's attempts to deal more realistically and effectively with the problem of economic insecurity.

The Industrial Revolution highlighted the problems associated with economic security. The change from a rural, agricultural, barter economy to an urban, industrial, money-wage economy resulted in dramatic and serious poverty when money wages stopped by reason of old age, unemployment, death, sickness, or other factors beyond the control of the individual. The modern family in an urban setting tends to be a parent-child family, with less close ties than in a rural economy to grandparents and grandchildren, uncles, aunts, nieces, and even adult brothers and sisters, and the large extended family has virtually disappeared. Economic insecurity, in the modern sense, was relatively unknown in primitive societies. However, as we conquered nature, developed industry, and an increasing proportion of our population became gainfully employed, the economic security of most persons and the necessities of life which could be purchased began to depend almost entirely upon the amount and steadiness of money income. Any interruption, stoppage, or reduction of income began to raise serious problems.

Although there are many reasons for economic insecurity in modern industrial society, five basic causes should be mentioned briefly since they represent risks to economic security which social security programs attempt to cover.

The Aged. In agricultural enterprises, the aged could be useful and employed so long as they could perform some work, whereas modern industry, with its rapid changes and mechanization, makes old age a handicap. As a result, only a small number of the aged can continue to work throughout their lifetime, even when physically able to do so, and very few have the kind of security that most of the aged have in an agricultural economy. For example, in 1890, 70 per cent of the men over 65 years of age in the United States were gainfully employed. By 1940, the number had decreased to 43 per cent, and by 1960 it was down to 34 per cent.

Furthermore, the vast majority of the aged reach old age without sufficient material resources to support themselves without working. At age 65 the life expectancy of men in the United States is about 13 years according to current mortality, and the life expectancy of women is about 16 years. The increased life expectancy at birth, combined with the gradual maturing of the age distribution of the population, has resulted in a total aged population (over 65) in the United States in 1962 of seventeen million, or 9.2 per cent of the United States population. The life expectancy at birth is higher today than ever before. In 1890, the life expectancy at birth of males in the United States was 40 years. By 1930 this life expectancy had increased to 58 years, and in 1960 the American male had an average life of 67 years. This increase in longevity is continuing as the standard of living continues to rise and modern medicine continues to decrease the impact of disease upon the life span.

The income of individuals declines sharply after 65 years of age, primarily because most persons are no longer employed at ages 65 and over. For those aged who are not full-time workers, most of the income comes from social insurance benefits. Men between 55 and 64 years of age had a median income in 1958 of $3,840, whereas men over 65 years of age had a median income of $1,440. Even among those gainfully employed as full-time, year-round workers, those over 65 had a median income of $3,560, whereas those between 55 and 64 years of age had a median income of $4,720.[7] From the discussion above, the situation is obvious. More people reach old age than ever before; as compared to past periods, a larger proportion of the aged are not gainfully employed, and the income of the aged is low.

The Unemployed. In many respects the most serious form of economic insecurity is due to unemployment. Not only is there a cessation of income when a person is unemployed, but frequently there is a loss of self-confidence on the part of the worker. Unemployment is caused by many factors: depressions, mechanization, seasonal occupations, business failures, individual inadequacies, or other personal reasons. But whatever the cause, the fact of unemployment increases the worker's psychological and economic insecurity.

Industrial Accident and Disease. Work has always presented certain hazards and dangers, but modern industry and the mechanization of agriculture have increased the risk to life and limb. In spite of a nation-wide campaign of industrial safety which has reduced work hazards in the United States, every year sees approximately two million persons disabled from work-connected disabilities. Such disabilities annually account for about 15,000 deaths, 1,500 total permanent disabilities, 83,000 partial permanent disabilities, and almost two million temporary disabilities.[8] Although the disability rates are lower than in many other industrial countries, the total number of persons affected is large, and such disabilities result in serious loss of income to workers and dependents, to say nothing of the personal, psychological, and other problems involved. It has been estimated that time lost from work in the United States due to work-connected disability is equivalent to 730,000 man-years.[9] There are 460 million restricted-activity days a year due to work-connected injuries alone.

Permanent Disability and Temporary Illness. On any one day almost two million persons in the United States labor force are unable to work because of some permanent disability or temporary illness. It has been estimated that in the year ending in June 1959, about ninety-three million activity-restricting acute conditions occurred among Americans aged 17 and over considered "usually working." These illnesses resulted in over 193 million work days lost.

While the frequency with which chronic conditions may occur is very much lower, the consequences of a chronic condition are, of course, likely to be very much more serious. Of the more than sixty-one million Americans aged 17 or over who were considered "usually working" in the year ending June 1959, almost one-half (over thirty million) had one or more chronic conditions. For almost five-and-a-half million "usually working" Americans these conditions resulted in some activity restriction. Almost four million were limited in their ability to work. Such conditions may result in temporary or permanent loss of income and at the same time increase the cost of living for the person affected because of medical and related expenditures.

Death. Although death rates are declining and death of the wage earner is a less important factor in producing economic insecurity than in previous periods, it is still a significant cause of cessation of family income. In January 1961 there were two million paternal orphans in the United States. In most of these instances the father's earnings had been the major source of the family's income. Today many widows are able to take over the role of family breadwinner and earn a living for themselves and their families when the husband dies. Where the widow is unable to work, however, because of her age or because she must remain at home to take care of her children, the income lost when the husband dies must be replaced by some form of nonwork income if the family is to remain intact.

EARLY ATTEMPTS TO ALLEVIATE ECONOMIC INSECURITY

The factors discussed above—old age, unemployment, disability, illness, industrial accident and disease, and death of the wage earner—have led to a variety of efforts to alleviate the resultant economic distress. Prior to the beginnings of social insurance around 1880, three major efforts were instituted by the industrial nations, particularly in Europe, to protect workers from destitution.[10] These three methods included a variety of savings plans, employers' liability, and private insurance.

To encourage workers to save, governments established government-operated savings banks, particularly in Western Europe. In the United States the early postal savings system was a comparable development. A large number of workers established savings accounts under government auspices and in many countries still maintain them. However, the low wages prior to 1900 were not conducive to saving, and illness, unemployment, accident, or old age frequently required far more money than the savings of a lifetime. As a method of insuring an individual's economic security, savings plans were uncertain, generally insufficient, and not very effective.[11]

The second method, based on the feudal system of relationship between the skilled worker and his apprentice who lived with him, was to place liability on the employer to care for the worker's family in case of death. This system is still in vogue in a few of the less industrialized countries of Latin America and the Middle East,[12] but has demonstrated its inadequacies to provide a broad program of economic security. The small employer finds it difficult to provide benefits; the risks are not widely distributed, thus falling heavily on a few; and there is always the problem of whether the death occurred within the strict legal limitations.

The third method of tackling the problem of economic insecurity was through a variety of private insurance schemes. A popular method prior to social insurance was the mutual aid society. One of the oldest was the Roman Collegia, which can be traced back to the founding of Rome.[13] It was an association of the common people organized primarily for fellowship and social activities, but it provided, through an "insurance" payment, for a funeral benefit. During the Middle Ages such mutual aid societies grew in number and influence. At first they were "labor guilds" which were later succeeded by another kind of mutual aid association—the Friendly Society—which spread rapidly among the working classes during the eighteenth and nineteenth centuries. In addition to funeral benefits they provided a variety of medical services. Some societies employed physicians to care for their members. By 1900, over five million persons were members of such societies in Great Britain alone.[14] In other European countries, mutual aid societies developed rapidly in cities and towns as industry expanded. The worker made a regular contribution to such societies, and benefits were paid to cover costs of his medical care and funeral expenses. As the mutual aid societies grew in size and importance, they came under government supervision and became similar to mutual insurance companies.

Mutual aid societies found that they could not extend benefits to cover retirement needs, nor could they provide extensive death benefits. As a result, a number of foreign governments in the latter half of the nineteenth century sponsored government insurance programs. For the most part they were unsuccessful except in one or two countries, such as Japan, where they enjoyed considerable popularity.

In Great Britain an insurance company developed "industrial insurance"—a plan which involved a small weekly payment to provide for funeral expenses and additional life insurance. Industrial insurance became popular in the United States, and millions of policies are today in force.

As a method of achieving economic security for the mass of workers, however, the effect of these early private insurance efforts was limited.

The methods described—personal savings, employers' liability, and private insurance—proved inadequate to keep workers from destitution. As industry expanded and unemployment, old age, death, disability, and sickness continued to cause serious hardships among workers, a demand arose for more satisfactory methods of assuring the worker that he would have some income when employment ceased.

THE BEGINNINGS OF SOCIAL INSURANCE

Prior to the twentieth century, widespread interest in providing a satisfactory and effective type of income security led to a variety of plans of "pooling the risk." In England, many writers urged a compulsory insurance program long before such plans were ever put into operation on a large scale in any country. Daniel Defoe advocated compulsory insurance for workers covering most of the risks protected by modern social insurance programs.[15] A proposal to combine the Friendly Societies into a national organization, to which persons in certain age and income groups would be required to contribute, was proposed by the Reverend John Acland of Devon in 1786.[16] His writings resulted in a bill being introduced into the House of Commons in 1787, but no action was taken on it. As early as 1831, the trade unions in England paid benefits to their unemployed members.[17] In 1893, the city of Berne, Switzerland, established a limited unemployment insurance program.

The City of Ghent, Belgium, subsidized the unemployment funds of labor unions in 1901, and the idea spread to many cities in other European countries. Although Belgium established voluntary old-age pensions in 1850 and France did likewise in 1851, the first compulsory social insurance system was adopted by Austria in 1854. Covering a limited number of workers for the risks of old age and invalidity, it was the subject of considerable interest.

The first comprehensive plan of social insurance began in Germany in the 1880's. The growth of industry was bringing wealth and power to the German nation; but at the same time the workers felt increasingly discontented with the recurring stoppage of income due primarily to unemployment, sickness, and old age. This discontent expressed itself in the rise of the Social Democrats and opposition to Chancellor Bismarck, the "Iron Chancellor." Bismarck saw in social insurance an opportunity to halt the rising tide of socialism by yielding to the workers' demands for income protection and, at the same time, to strengthen the central German government as opposed to the states and local governmental units. He proposed a national plan of workmen's accident insurance in 1881, and for the next seven or eight years Bismarck's proposals covering other risks were vigorously debated in Germany and, indeed, throughout the world.

In 1883, Germany adopted a program of compulsory insurance against illness; accident insurance followed in 1884; and compulsory invalidity and old-age insurance was begun in 1889.[18] The German social insurance programs laid the groundwork for social insurance programs of many other countries. Many of its basic concepts were similar to those of the social insurance system of the United States. The system was based on contributions made by workers, employers, and the government. Reserve funds were established, and the money collected, after deducting current expenses and benefit payments, was placed in reserves from which funds were to be drawn whenever current receipts were insufficient to meet current expenditures. The contributions or taxes were wage-related; that is, the higher the wage, the greater the contribution or tax. Benefits were also wage-related. The system was compulsory and coverage was widespread.

The establishment of such broad social insurance programs in Germany accelerated the movement toward "income security" programs in other countries. It is interesting, however, that the German system, the basic concepts of which are now predominant features of most current social insurance programs, did not meet with immediate favor in other countries. Particularly with reference to old age, other countries adopted programs which might be called "social assistance" as distinguished from "social insurance."

Denmark studied the problems of replacing income lost or not available by reason of old age and rejected the approach of social insurance. In 1891, it established a program of "pensions" to needy aged over 60 years of age, and national law required local authorities to make payments which, although the amounts were not specified, were to be sufficient to maintain the aged person and his family.[19] These pensions were to be paid from general tax revenues without the special contributions or earmarked taxes that were inherent in the German social insurance program.

Following Denmark's lead, other countries established programs of social assistance with benefits payable from general public revenues on the basis of legal right to such benefits to needy persons in prescribed amounts. Social assistance programs spread chiefly to other Scandinavian countries and to English-speaking countries.[20] New Zealand established pensions for needy aged in 1898, and Great Britain and Australia did so in 1908. Limited at first to old age, such pension programs were later extended to other groups, such as invalids, survivors, and the unemployed.

Social assistance programs are of two types: either a flat pension, or a grant based on "need." In the former, as an example, every person 65 years of age or over (or other established age) receives the same payment; in the latter, the payments would vary according to the need of the individual. For example, an ill person who required a special diet might receive more than one who did not have such needs.

For the past fifty years, proponents of social insurance and social assistance have argued the merits of each approach. Social assistance advocates contend that either a flat pension or an amount based on the need of the individual is more equitable in that the funds come from general revenues and therefore the burden can be more equitably distributed. Furthermore, a payroll tax (such as in social insurance) is a regressive tax, falling most heavily on low-income workers. A social assistance program, it is held, is more flexible; it can be changed more readily, since there is no implied commitment for specific payments as there might be when workers make social insurance contributions. They argue further that the social insurance concept is a fiction, that workers are not really insured, that benefits can be changed or terminated by national legislatures, and that persons making contributions frequently do not pay enough to warrant calling the benefits an insurance payment.

On the other hand, the social insurance advocates point to the rapid growth of the program throughout the world. Many persons early began to look upon pensions as established in Denmark as a form of charity even when not based strictly on need. Compulsory earmarked payroll taxes, moreover, constitute a feasible method of raising the necessary revenues, and the fact that under most social insurance systems each worker makes a payment has an important psychological implication. The worker feels that he is saving for his old age or other risk and therefore has a greater interest in the program's soundness. Social assistance, dependent on current revenues to defray costs, might well become unable to meet mounting costs in a depression when general tax revenues decline. Under social insurance, reserves can be built up to tide over such depression periods. Furthermore, the hardships caused by stoppage of income do not fall equally on all persons. A worker averaging $400 a month in wages will find it more difficult to live on a pension of $100 per month than a worker averaging $200 in wages. Under social insurance, benefits can be "wage-related"; that is, the higher the average wages, the higher the benefit.

The United States has adopted both approaches. Its social security system includes social insurance covering the risks of industrial accident and disease, old age, permanent and total disability, and death; and social assistance schemes for persons whose needs are not met through social insurance.

Whether a country used the social insurance or social assistance approach, the basic idea of protection against loss of income spread rapidly, and by 1930 practically every country in Europe, as well as almost every other industrialized nation, had some type of program.

Today the United States has many programs to protect individuals against loss of income, and economic security for all Americans is a basic goal of public social policy in the United States. A variety of methods and programs to achieve the goal have been instituted. Governmental and voluntary programs, social insurance and private insurance, pensions and public assistance or relief, individual savings, home ownership—these and other factors have combined to increase the economic security of most Americans.

For example, Congress enacted the Employment Act of 1946, which constitutes action by the Federal government to maintain full employment and to keep people at work. The efforts of the present administration under President John F. Kennedy to assist areas of chronic unemployment are likewise in this category. To find jobs for workers and workers for jobs, an extensive system of state-administered public employment offices was promoted by the Congressional enactment of the Wagner-Peyser Act of 1933. In the Federal Government, the Bureau of Employment Security in the United States Department of Labor assists and co-ordinates the state employment offices, prescribes standards of efficiency, and encourages uniformity in administrative and statistical procedures for these state systems. The Bureau acts as a clearinghouse for employment opportunities among the various states. Safety programs to reduce industrial accidents also are preventive in nature. In this respect, the American industrial safety program is one of the best in the world. For example, industrial deaths in 1913 were 25,000 and in 1955 approximately 14,200, in spite of the fact that population during this period of time more than doubled.

Public service programs such as institutions for the aged, the mentally ill, and veterans are illustrative of a host of public service programs which assist in maintaining the income security of the American people. One of the most important of these public service programs is that of vocational rehabilitation. Industrial accidents and crippling diseases during the latter part of the nineteenth century resulted in a variety of voluntary and governmental efforts to rehabilitate disabled persons and place them back into productive employment. A number of voluntary efforts, including workshops and rehabilitation centers, were established between 1890 and 1920.

Following World War I, the Federal Government established a rehabilitation program for disabled veterans, and in 1920 Congress passed the Vocational Rehabilitation Act, which made available Federal funds to each state for the purpose of providing vocational training and job placement for disabled civilians. In 1935, the Social Security Act established a national program of vocational rehabilitation, which is now administered by the Vocational Rehabilitation Administration of the United States Department of Health, Education, and Welfare. In 1943, the Barden-LaFollette Act expanded and improved the Federal Government's vocational rehabilitation program. The Vocational Rehabilitation Administration assists the states in developing and providing state-operated vocational rehabilitation services to assist physically and mentally handicapped persons to achieve the independence and dignity associated with productive employment in accordance with their individual capacities. Federal funds are available as grants-in-aid to the states for services necessary for the vocational rehabilitation of disabled persons, including medical study and diagnosis, medical, surgical, and hospital care, prosthetic devices, counselling and guidance, training for specific occupations or skills, service in comprehensive or specialized rehabilitation facilities, tools required for jobs, job placement, and related services. The Vocational Rehabilitation Administration, in addition to making grants to states for the rehabilitation of disabled individuals, makes grants to governmental and voluntary agencies for research and demonstration projects in the field of vocational rehabilitation. The basic goal of the vocational rehabilitation program is that of rehabilitating disabled persons so that disability shall not stand in the way of appropriate employment.

Many voluntary and private resources also assist in the maintenance of economic security. Private industrial pension programs will be discussed later. Covering as they do many million workers, they contribute significantly to economic security.

"America has grappled with the problem of security, sometimes with an inventiveness that has added to the European experience instead of merely imitating it." [21] —*Max Lerner*

CHAPTER III

EARLY BEGINNINGS IN THE UNITED STATES

Prior to 1930, the pressure to insure against the risks of unemployment, old age, and sickness was not so great in the United States as in European countries. The American frontier kept expanding during the entire one hundred years of the nineteenth century. Land was given to settlers by the government either free or for a nominal charge. The frontier was opulent—rich forests, minerals, and agricultural lands provided the American worker who left the industrial Eastern seaboard with his "social security" for over a century.

Under laws passed in the early nineteenth century, every head of a family or single person over 21 years of age could enter upon and "homestead" a quarter section (160 acres).[22] In the desert such persons could acquire 320 acres. With small improvements and a short period of residence, the land became the sole and private property of the homesteader.

This homestead policy was in large degree responsible for the tremendous growth and prosperity of the United States prior to 1900. For fifty years, from 1850 to 1900, an average of six million acres or 35,000 farms per year were added to the improved and cultivated areas of the United States.[23]

While the frontier provided great economic opportunities, the city worker began to feel the insecurities of unemployment, old age, and sickness. Mutual aid societies and fraternal orders sprang up offering to their members funeral, sickness, and old-age benefits. These efforts served a useful purpose but were ineffective in solving the problems presented in the rapidly industrializing and ever-expanding economy of the United States.

In the meantime the public welfare and private relief agencies continued to expand. The English Elizabethan poor laws were adopted in the United States soon after it established itself as a nation, along with their principles of local responsibility, the liability of relatives for support of indigent members of the family, and residence laws which restricted eligibility for relief to residents of the locality. The care of the "poor," therefore, was accepted as a governmental responsibility since the founding of the country. However, local governmental agencies were loath to assist the new immigrants. From 1850 to 1920, millions of Europeans poured into the United States, bringing with them hope for a new life but very few worldly goods. It fell to the lot of the voluntary relief societies to care for such groups.

The lack of a comprehensive public program or plan to provide economic security was not due to neglect or indifference. It reflected an important and affirmative American philosophy: a philosophy which placed on the individual the responsibility for his own welfare. Nevertheless, the fact of economic insecurity—the clear evidence of poverty and suffering—was shattering the faith of many in the ability of persons to take care of themselves.

By the beginning of the twentieth century, agitation for more orderly and adequate solutions to the problems of destitution and stoppage of income became widespread. The large number of industrial accidents resulted in demands for some kind of insurance against industrial accident and disease, similar to the program in Germany. In 1902 the state of Maryland passed the first workmen's compensation law, but it was declared unconstitutional. The court held that such a law, which provided a system of compulsory insurance, deprived the worker of his common law rights to sue the employer as guaranteed by the Constitution.[24]

Such decisions fanned public indignation, and a strong popular demand arose for workmen's compensation legislation similar to that established in Europe. This demand was eloquently voiced by President Theodore Roosevelt, who declared in 1907: ". . . it is revolting to judgment and sentiment alike that the financial burden of accidents occurring because of the necessary exigencies of their daily occupation should be thrust upon those sufferers who are least able to bear it."[25]

Under the leadership of the President, Congress enacted in May

908 the first workmen's compensation law which successfully withstood attacks on its constitutionality. The act covered civil employ-
es of the Federal Government. With Federal leadership pointing
he way, the states soon followed suit. Between 1910 and 1915,
hirty states enacted compensation laws,[26] and today all states have
such legislation.

While the social insurance program of workmen's compensation
was spreading throughout the country in the first quarter of this
century, a companion social assistance movement for old-age pensions was also making headway.

Public relief programs failed to meet the demand by the American people for adequate security for the growing number of destitute aged. Many such aged were being housed in almshouses or
county poor farms. In 1914, Arizona established the first noncontributory old-age pension system in the United States. The law
was poorly drawn and was declared unconstitutional by the Arizona court.[27] However, the movement made great headway and
later laws were approved by the courts.

By 1931, seventeen states and Alaska had passed laws providing
assistance for aged persons not in institutions who were "needy."
These laws were generally referred to as "old-age pension laws." [28]
Only Delaware assumed all of the cost on a state basis. In eleven
states all costs were assumed by local governments; in the remainder, states and local communities shared the costs.

These old-age-pension laws accelerated the movement toward
old-age insurance.[29] In general they were merely a liberalization of
the traditional poor laws. Eligibility to such old-age pensions generally depended on the aged person being destitute, having long
residence in the state, and not having relatives able or willing to
support him.

The European experience in social insurance schemes had ardent
American advocates. In 1912, Dr. I. M. Rubinow,[30] a Doctor of
Medicine, was asked to give a course in "Social Insurance" at the
New York School of Philanthropy. Following Dr. Rubinow's initial
effort, several courses appeared under this title in American universities.[31] The next year, Dr. Rubinow published the first comprehensive American study of social insurance. Numerous efforts were
made to organize popular support for a social insurance program,

and a number of significant writers appeared. Barbara Armstrong, one of the first women professors in a major law school (University of California), wrote a number of articles, culminating in a book in 1932,[32] which had a significant impact on many of the persons who shortly thereafter participated in establishing the United States social security program.

Two main streams of thinking and resultant political pressure were making headway prior to 1932: one group was promoting social insurance; the other, flat pensions. Perhaps the most vocal spokesman of the former group was Abraham Epstein. In 1927 he had organized the American Association for Old Age Security, later changed to the American Association for Social Security. His writings and articles stirred interest throughout the country. His book, published in 1933,[33] sounded a ringing call to action.

The second movement which influenced the later course of events was the Townsend movement. This movement was started by Dr. Francis E. Townsend, a physician, in Long Beach, California, in 1933. He proposed a flat pension of $200 per month for all persons aged sixty and over.[34] His plan was to be financed by a Federal sales tax. The movement spread rapidly, and within two years there were 4,550 Townsend Clubs throughout the country. These two movements added to the impetus of the later New Deal programs—the Civilian Conservation Corps (CCC), the Federal Emergency Relief programs, and the various Federal work programs—to provide a climate favorable to the establishment of America's social security program.

"We are moving forward to greater freedom, to greater security for the average man than he has ever known before in the history of America." [35] —*Franklin D. Roosevelt*

CHAPTER IV

THE GREAT DEPRESSION AND THE BATTLE FOR SOCIAL SECURITY

The growth of America's industrial effort and the diminishing economic effect of the expanding frontier made the problems of employment and unemployment increasingly important in the total picture of economic security. Widespread unemployment in the depression of 1906 and the resultant suffering and misery among industrial workers, however, was almost forgotten after World War I as the United States moved ahead into unprecedented prosperity. New fortunes were created; great business empires were built or expanded; and the voices of social reformers such as Jane Addams, Abraham Epstein, Harold Ickes, and Donald Richberg were lost in the approval given by the optimism and praise of American business. Many felt that the nation had reached "a permanent plateau of prosperity." [36] Stocks on the New York Stock Exchange reached an all-time high in the summer of 1929 and the American people generally echoed President Hoover's faith in America's future as being "bright with hope." [37]

There were, however, many disturbing signs. In the summer of 1928, private welfare agencies noted that the number of persons needing financial assistance because of unemployment continued to rise, although in previous years the number had usually decreased in the summer period. Residential construction also slowed down in 1929, and business inventories more than tripled.

On October 23, the unexpected occurred and stock prices began falling. Within a few weeks, stocks on the New York Stock Exchange had lost 40 per cent of their value.[38]

Although the President and business leaders continued to issue statements reflecting their earlier optimism, these statements did not reflect the feeling of the man in the street. Unemployment mounted. In December 1930, the Metropolitan Life Insurance Company made a survey of its industrial policyholders in forty-six cities and reported that 23.8 per cent were wholly unemployed and an additional 21.3 per cent were employed only part-time.[39] Some students estimated that the unemployed reached twelve-and-a-half million.

Such widespread unemployment on a national scale and the resulting large-scale destitution was a new experience for the United States. Workers exhausted their savings, and soon credit sources dried up. The neighborhood grocer could not "carry" the growing number of destitute; stores closed; many lost their farms and homes due to foreclosures; fear of the future was rampant; and for the first time in many years bread lines were seen in every major city.

American leaders, unprepared for such a catastrophe, frequently added to the growing confusion and despair. Senator Robert F. Wagner of New York proposed in 1930 and 1931 a comprehensive national employment service, while many Federal officials maintained that unemployment was strictly a local responsibility. When social workers like Clarence Pickett of the Friends Service Committee and Lillian Wald of the Henry Street Settlement demanded Federal assistance, President Hoover maintained that voluntary organizations could care for the unemployed. Colonel Arthur Woods (Chairman of President Hoover's first committee for employment) proposed a public works program involving slum clearance and low-cost housing, while Walter S. Gifford, Chairman of Hoover's second committee (the President's Committee on Unemployment Relief), emphasized the beneficence of charity and private philanthropy.

As destitution increased, voluntary agencies soon exhausted all of their resources. Local governments organized soup kitchens and spread their meager funds thinly over the growing numbers demanding assistance. Conservative farmers in the Middle West, seeing their farms jeopardized through foreclosures, and many conservatives in the American Federation of Labor, seeing their members reduced to a starvation existence, openly talked of revolt, while Richard Whitney of the New York Stock Exchange urged that we do nothing and let nature take its course.[40] Many insisted on Federal aid to business but deplored talk about Federal aid to the destitute.

By 1932 the situation had become desperate. The lingering hope that the relief of distress could be handled by local and voluntary agencies faded. Federal leaders and the President finally agreed to assist business through the organization of the Reconstruction Finance Corporation (RFC) but continued their opposition to any assistance directly to the unemployed.

In the fall of 1931, New York State established the first "state emergency relief" program to assist local units to dispense unemployment relief. By March 1932, seven states were financing relief to the unemployed.[41] But the states were finding it difficult to cope with the problem and began demanding Federal assistance.

Reluctantly, President Hoover agreed that the RFC would expand its functions to provide advances to states for relief and loans for public works projects—such advances and loans to be repaid by the states. This program, established pursuant to the Emergency Relief and Construction Act of 1932 (passed July 1932) stimulated the establishment of state emergency relief administrations in an additional thirty-three states.[42]

In the Presidential elections of 1932, the question of Federal relief became a campaign issue. Franklin Delano Roosevelt, as Governor of New York, had sponsored the first state emergency relief program, and in his Presidential campaign he urged Federal participation in relief programs, public works, and unemployment insurance.

Franklin Delano Roosevelt became President on March 4, 1933. In his view, the election was a clear mandate to use the powers of the Federal Government to remedy the situation. One of the most controversial moves of the new administration was the injection of the Federal Government into the problem of relief. Many business and political leaders, who eagerly sought Federal intervention and assistance to aid banks, agriculture, industry, and various commercial enterprises, found it difficult to accept similar assistance to the destitute. President Roosevelt, on March 21, 1933, sent a message to Congress recommending that a Federal Relief Administration be established. A few days later a bill was introduced, and it was passed within a few weeks to provide grants to states and localities for relief purposes. The bill passed the Senate by a vote of 55 to 17 and the House of Representatives by a vote of 326 to 42. The Federal Government thereby embarked on a new phase of national policy—the relief of destitution became a responsibility of the Federal Government.

The legislation, known as the Federal Emergency Relief Act of 1933, provided grants to states for relief of destitution. Its funds were used both for direct relief and for work relief; i.e., persons were paid for work on public projects. Half of the Federal funds were used to match state funds; for every dollar of Federal funds granted, the states were required to spend three dollars from their own sources. The remaining half of the Federal money was appropriated at the discretion of the Federal Government without the necessity for matching.

The Federal Emergency Relief Administration (FERA) was headed by Harry Hopkins, who had been President Roosevelt's administrator of the New York Temporary Emergency Relief Administration when Roosevelt was Governor. A social worker with a dedication to the cause of the underprivileged, he brought to the task a knowledge of the problems of poverty, boundless energy, and unusual organizing ability.

Under his leadership a variety of programs assisted several million persons. Although immediate assistance to the destitute took the form of direct relief, Hopkins urged states to establish work-relief programs. Other programs followed. In April 1934, a special program to rehabilitate farm families was launched. This program, known as the Rural Rehabilitation Program, provided work relief to rural families, advice on agricultural problems, and farm loans. The Rural Rehabilitation Program was absorbed in 1935 by the Resettlement Administration, later the Farm Security Administration. A special program to aid transients, i.e., persons who did not have local or state residence, was also instituted. A student-aid program made grants to colleges for employment of needy students. Encouraged by financial assistance from FERA, thousands of self-help and co-operative associations were formed by the unemployed, to produce products for sale or consumption by the members.

The FERA program had an immediate impact on the unemployed and assisted in alleviating the hardships of widespread unemployment. Other programs, meanwhile, were contributing to this end also. The Civilian Conservation Corps (CCC) provided jobs for more than two million unemployed young men on projects concerned with forestry and wild life. In October 1933, a Federal Surplus Relief Corporation was established. It purchased surplus foods from farmers and distributed them to the needy. Such foods were in addition to regular relief grants. This surplus food program served two purposes: it maintained the income of farmers and provided food for the needy.

A series of work programs characterized the early efforts of the New Deal. In June 1933, the Public Works Administration was organized to stimulate large public works projects. Loans were made to states for public works as well as grants which were matched by state funds. However, the necessity for careful preliminary planning of large projects caused this program to start slowly, and its impact on unemployment was not substantial for the first year or two.

The slowness of the Public Works Administration program, and the difficulties involved in forty-eight separate state work-relief programs, led Hopkins to recommend a national work program. In November 1933, the Civil Works Administration (CWA) was established. In two months (January 1934) over four million persons were at work. Although it was terminated in July 1934, it made a significant contribution. Over 400,000 projects were started. In a few months, 500,000 miles of roads were built or repaired; 40,000 schools were built or improved; 500 new airports were established; parks, sewers, firebreaks, irrigation ditches, forestry trails, and public buildings were started or improved—these were merely indicative of the wide variety and scope of this public works program.

The success of the CWA established work relief as a desirable program in the minds of Congressional leaders. However, the high cost due to its speed of organization resulted in considerable criticism, and pressure arose for a more orderly and long-range work-relief program. In April 1935, Congress authorized funds for a work-relief program to employ three-and-a-half million employable persons.[43] As a result, the Works Progress Administration, later known as the Work Projects Administration (WPA), was created.

It was the largest of the New Deal relief programs and employed a total of over eight million persons from 1935 to 1940.

By the middle of 1934, many national leaders, both in and out of government, became convinced of the necessity of a comprehensive Federal program of social insurance or public assistance or both. A number of factors accounted for this conviction—a conviction which expressed a profound change in thinking from previous periods when American leadership opposed Federal programs in the economic security field. The Depression highlighted the problem of economic insecurity. One authority doubted "very much whether [the Social Security Act] or any similar measure could have passed, at least for many years, had it come before Congress later than 1935." [44] By 1934, there was a general acceptance of governmental responsibility for all types of relief. As early as 1912 the Progressive Party had urged old-age pensions, and more than thirty states had such programs by 1934. In addition, many had established mothers' pension programs to assist widows and orphaned children. Furthermore, the participation of the Federal Government in relief programs for the first time emphasized the national nature of destitution and economic insecurity. The numerous New Deal programs made a tremendous impact on the American people and resulted in a feeling that the beneficial aspects of these programs should be preserved in some permanent program.

The groundwork for a permanent program had been established since the FERA and related projects necessitated well-organized state welfare agencies to administer Federal grants. Each state established or improved its state welfare department or welfare services. As a result, every local area had some public welfare office, and the nation was, therefore, better equipped than ever before to handle a nationally established program. As previously indicated, the Townsend movement was resulting in strong pressures for a Federal old-age-pension program. Also of major importance was the changing philosophy of the American people and their leaders. The concept that poverty was the result of improvidence, laziness, and general unworthiness did not square with the evidence available for all to see, namely, that millions of hard-working, industrious, and hitherto economically independent workers were unable to find jobs through circumstances completely outside of their individual control.

Finally, the movement for social insurance was growing. Workmen's compensation had been established in practically all states. The Democratic Party platform of 1932 advocated "unemployment and old-age insurance." Bills had been introduced in several state legislatures in the 1920's providing for some form of unemployment insurance. Wisconsin had established an unemployment insurance program, and its operation gave impetus to the efforts of social insurance advocates.

In June 1934, President Roosevelt appointed the "Committee on Economic Security" [45] as a first step to implement his promise that he intended to recommend measures to protect Americans from the risks which caused destitution and dependency. The Committee consisted of the Secretary of Labor as Chairman, the Secretary of the Treasury, the Attorney General, the Secretary of Agriculture, and the Federal Emergency Relief Administrator.[46] The Committee was charged with the responsibility of studying and recommending legislation which would promote the economic security of the individual. The Executive Order also established three other bodies. An Advisory Council on Economic Security composed of twenty-three leading citizens was established to give advice to the Cabinet committee. The committee consisted of business and industrial leaders, labor union officials, social workers, educators, farm and other public representatives. Another body was the Technical Board of Economic Security, composed of individuals within the government service and charged with the responsibility of technical studies. Arthur J. Altmeyer, Assistant Secretary of Labor (later Commissioner for Social Security), was Chairman of the Technical Board and was assisted by twenty top Federal officials and eight advisory committees.[47]

Finally, an Executive Director was appointed. He had complete charge of all studies and served as secretary of all three committees. The Executive Director, Dr. Edwin E. Witte, Professor of Economics at the University of Wisconsin, had been a student of social insurance and a recognized authority in the field. Every known student of, or specialist in, social insurance or related programs was approached to become a staff member employed on a full- or part-time basis.[48] In addition, a two-day National Conference on Social Security was called in November 1934 which brought together several hundred people interested in social security.

Within a few months the Committee on Economic Security completed the most comprehensive study and analysis of social insurance and social assistance which had ever been undertaken in the United States. The studies included experience in other countries as well as in the United States, an analysis of various private insurance programs, and fiscal and administrative problems.[49] Although there were many differences of opinion within the Committee, the Advisory Board, and the Technical Staff, the final Report of the Committee on Economic Security (January 15, 1935)[50] represented a bold and imaginative departure from the past and laid the groundwork for a comprehensive program of social security in the United States.

The Committee recommended legislation covering a variety of subjects. Its chief recommendations may be classified under four heads:

1. A threefold program to assure economic security for the aged. This included:

    (a) A Federally administered plan of compulsory old-age annuities.[51]

    (b) A voluntary government plan of old-age annuities.[52]

    (c) Federal grants-in-aid to states establishing an old-age assistance program based on a needs test.[53]

2. A Federal-state program of unemployment insurance.[54]

3. Federal grants-in-aid to the states to provide assistance to widows and surviving children and child welfare services.[55a]

4. Extension of Public Health Services.[55b]

On January 17, 1935, President Roosevelt transmitted the Report of the Committee on Economic Security to Congress, and in his special message urged quick action to enact into law its principal recommendations.

On that day, Senator Wagner of New York introduced the Administration bill in the Senate,[56] and Representatives Lewis and Doughton introduced it in the House of Representatives.[57] These bills had as their short titles "The Economic Security Act."

Extensive public hearings were held by the Finance Committee of the Senate[58] and the Ways and Means Committee of the House of Representatives.[59] At these hearings, in the later debates on the floor of both Houses, and in the public press, feeling ran high. Business leaders generally saw in old-age insurance the destruction of "individual initiative and thrift" while supporters of the program saw in it a new "happiness in old age for America's aged." Opponents of unemployment insurance feared that "no one would work," while proponents maintained that it would save American industry from collapse.

Although hearings were completed quickly by the middle of February, it was the middle of April before the House Ways and Means Committee reported out a bill. It called the bill the Social Security Act.[60] This was the first use of the words "social security" in the legislation of any country. On April 19, the bill passed the House; on June 19 it passed the Senate; in August, the Conference Committee of both Houses reconciled certain differences in the Senate and House versions; and the President signed the Social Security Act on August 14, 1935.[61] Unfortunately, Senator Huey Long conducted a successful filibuster which prevented an appropriation of funds with which to begin operations. The President, however, made funds available from the NRA and WPA until the next session of Congress [62] and personnel were borrowed from other agencies to begin work.

Shortly after President Roosevelt signed the Act, he appointed the first Social Security Board. As Chairman, he named John G. Winant, former Governor of New Hampshire and later United States Ambassador to Great Britain; the other members were Arthur J. Altmeyer, later Chairman of the Board (1937–1946) and Commissioner for Social Security (1946–1953), and Vincent Morgan Miles, an Arkansas lawyer.

The Social Security Act as finally passed did not encompass all of the recommendations of the Committee on Economic Security. The proposal for a voluntary government program offering old-age annuities for sale in competition with private insurance companies was not enacted. Further, the Committee had favored in principle a state-administered system of health insurance supervised by the Federal Government on a grant-in-aid basis, but the speed with which the Committee worked resulted in a lack of specific recommendations to the President on this point.[63] Nevertheless, the Act adopted the basic recommendations of the Committee. It established a Federally administered compulsory old-age-insurance program (actually called "Old-Age Benefits");[64] grants to states for old-age assistance;[65] a state-operated system of unemployment insurance;[66] grants to states for needy dependent children;[67] grants to states for maternal and child welfare;[68] grants to states for aid to the blind;[69] and other provisions.

The Act of 1935 has been amended frequently during the twenty-seven years of its operation. Major amendments were made in 1939, 1946, 1950, 1952, 1954, 1956, 1958, 1960, 1961, and 1962.[70]

The enactment of the Social Security Act and its approval by the President did not stop the battle against social security. Even many friends of the program had considerable doubt as to whether the Act would be upheld by the courts as an appropriate exercise of Federal legislative power.

It was not until 1937 that the Supreme Court of the United States upheld the constitutionality of the Social Security Act. The first case to come before the Court challenged the constitutionality of the unemployment insurance program.[71] It was contended, among other things, that the tax levied was arbitrary and not uniform, that it invaded the reserved powers of the states, and that the states had abandoned governmental functions which they had no power to abandon. Justice Cardozo delivered the opinion of the Court holding the Act constitutional. On the same day, the Court handed down another opinion holding the old-age-insurance provisions of the Act constitutional.[72] This latter decision clearly enunciated the principle of Federal interest in old-age pensions and asserted the doctrine that changing conditions demand changing programs. Said Justice Cardozo in this decision:

"Nor is the concept of the general welfare static. Needs that were narrow or parochial a century ago may be interwoven in our day with the well-being of the nation. What is critical or urgent changes with the times."

Asserting that the problem of the aged is "plainly national in area and dimensions" and that the "laws of the separate states cannot deal with it effectively," the Court contended that "Congress may spend money in and for the general welfare" and that "only a power that is national can serve the interests of all."

With this decision a new phase began in the history of the Federal Government's activities to relieve destitution and establish social welfare programs. It involved a major change in United States policy and a significant break with past restrictions and inhibitions.[73] It laid the groundwork for the gradual development of the largest public welfare program of the western world. This program emphasizes economic security for the people of the United States as an important national goal.

Economic security has not been and will perhaps never be fully achieved by any society. Nevertheless, significant beginnings have been made in the United States through a variety of measures and economic arrangements. Primary emphasis has been on employment and wages or compensation to assure a decent standard of living. American mores and beliefs have emphasized self-reliance, have encouraged individual initiative to plan for the individual's own security, and have resulted in the accumulation of real and personal property resources to aid in meeting economic contingencies. Substantial home ownership, life insurance, savings, and other assets form part of the economic security of millions of Americans.

Social security has been adopted in the United States because of the realization (which came later than in Europe) that wages can and do stop when certain contingencies arise, that many persons find themselves destitute for reasons beyond their control, and that certain governmental programs and services are essential to assist the individual in his own efforts to achieve support and economic and social independence.

A variety of industrial programs also assist in making life more secure for many workers. Industrial pension plans now add to and supplement social security, and many industries are providing life insurance, sickness benefits, health insurance, medical care, and other social services for their workers. It is this four-pronged approach of (1) employment and adequate compensation, (2) individual initiative resulting in privately accumulated financial resources, (3) social security, and (4) industrial pensions and other services which forms the cornerstone of our economic security program.

"With the Social Security Act the constitutional dedication of Federal power to the general welfare began a new phase of national history." [74]—*Arthur M. Schlesinger, Jr.*

CHAPTER V

OLD-AGE, SURVIVORS, AND
DISABILITY INSURANCE

The largest program under the Social Security Act is Old-Age, Survivors, and Disability Insurance (OASDI). About seventeen million persons received benefits under this program in April 1962 at an annual benefit rate of almost thirteen billion dollars. The program has influenced and shaped the philosophy, concepts, and direction of all social security programs in the United States. Generally, when the average American speaks of his "social security," he means old-age, survivors, and disability insurance.

Old-age, survivors, and disability insurance is a Federally operated program administered by the Social Security Administration. This Administration is headed by a "Commissioner of Social Security" appointed by the President and is part of the Department of Health, Education, and Welfare; the Secretary of Health, Education, and Welfare is a Cabinet officer. The old-age, survivors, and disability insurance program provides protection to workers and their families against loss or stoppage of earnings resulting from retirement in old age, death, and disability.

The program is financed by taxes paid by employers and employees in those employments covered by the Act, the tax being on the earnings or wages of the employee. Self-employed persons likewise pay a tax on their earnings. The tax rate is set by Congress, in an amount intended to be sufficient over the long-range future to enable the program to pay the benefits provided when they fall due. Funds not needed for current benefit payments and administrative expenses are accumulated in two trust funds, which are invested in interest-bearing securities of the United States Government. More than 90 per cent of those gainfully employed in the

United States are covered by the system or are eligible for coverage.

Persons who work long enough in covered employment become insured. When a person acquires insured status, four types of benefits may become payable, based on his earnings record:

1. The worker himself may receive old-age benefits when he retires at age 62 or later, or he may get disability benefits if he retires prior to age 62 because of permanent and total disability.

2. Benefits may be paid to certain dependents of the retired or disabled worker.

3. Benefits may be paid to certain survivors of a deceased worker (including deceased retired workers), and

4. A lump-sum payment may be made upon death of a worker.

Benefits are paid monthly without regard to a person's need. Benefits are based on the worker's average monthly earnings, with a higher percentage of the average monthly wage being paid to the lower earnings group. If the worker receiving benefits earns through employment or self-employment an amount over the limit established, his benefit may be reduced or completely withheld.

As previously indicated, the program was established by the passage of the Social Security Act on August 14, 1935. There have been ten major revisions in amendments passed by Congress. The discussion following will describe the program as it is today as a result of these amendments.

BASIC CONCEPTS

In common with the social security programs of most countries, the United States program of old-age, survivors, and disability insurance is based on detailed and complicated statutory provisions and administrative regulations. However, the program may be described and discussed around its ten basic concepts or premises, and each of these ten aspects will be discussed separately in the sections to follow.

1. Coverage

A basic premise and goal of the old-age, survivors, and disability insurance program is that all persons who work, regardless of income level, type of employment, citizenship, age, or other special characteristic, should be covered by the system. This goal of universal coverage is on the way to achievement. All gainfully employed are covered, whether employees or self-employed, unless specifically excluded by law. "Coverage" refers to the type of employment, the earnings from which are subject to a social security tax and which earnings will entitle the person so employed to receive the various social security benefits. To be eligible for benefits a person must acquire insured status. This is acquired by employment in work specified by the Social Security Act for a specified number of calendar quarters (a quarter is a three-month period beginning January 1, April 1, July 1, or October 1) in which the individual has received $50 or more in wages. Self-employed persons are covered only if they have net self-employment income of $400 or more in a year, and then they are generally credited with four quarters of coverage. Agricultural workers receive one quarter of coverage for each full $100 of covered wages received in a year (up to a maximum of four quarters of coverage per year—the maximum number of quarters which can be counted under any circumstances). "Employment," therefore, is a key concept in coverage, and those employments excluded and included should be mentioned briefly.

The major groups excluded from coverage are: Federal civilian employees if they are covered under a retirement system, self-employed physicians (doctors of medicine), some employees of state and local governments, clergymen and ministers who do not elect to be covered, certain domestic and agricultural workers (although most are covered), employees of some nonprofit organizations who have not arranged for coverage for their employees (most are covered), employees of Communist-action or Communist-front organizations who register under the Internal Security Act of 1950 or are ordered to register by the Subversive Activities Control Board, low-income self-employed persons (income under $400 per year), and railroad workers, who have their own governmental system which is closely co-ordinated with old-age, survivors, and disability insurance.

For practical purposes, then, almost all gainfully employed persons are covered by the old-age, survivors, and disability insurance system, or are eligible for coverage, or are under another governmental retirement system. About nine-tenths of the nation's workers and self-employed are covered and about the same number of the nation's children and their mothers have survivorship protection that assures them of a monthly income if the family breadwinner were to die.

The original Social Security Act followed the pattern of many other countries and limited coverage to wage earners in industry and commerce, practically all of whom were covered. Although many countries still restrict coverage to wage earners in industry and commerce, the United States has extended coverage to almost all of those originally excluded.

The 1950 amendments to the Social Security Act brought in categories of work for which coverage appeared too difficult in the beginning. These amendments covered most types of regularly employed agricultural labor. Under the 1954 amendments, coverage was extended to self-employed farmers. Today, most types of farming and agricultural labor are covered. Self-employed farmers are covered if their earnings amount to $400 or more in a year. Because the Congress did not want to require low-income farmers to keep financial records which they ordinarily did not maintain, an alternative method for determining net earnings was established. If the farmer's gross income is $1,800 or less, the farmer may elect to count as "net earnings" for purposes of social security taxes and benefits either his actual net earnings or two-thirds of the gross. For example, if the gross is $1,500, expenses were $1,100, and net earnings, therefore, were $400, the farmer may count the $400 as his social security earnings, or alternatively may report two-thirds of the gross income of $1,500, which would be $1,000, to be counted as his social security earnings. If the farmer has a gross farm income of more than $1,800 with a net of less than $1,200, then the farmer may count either the actual net earnings or $1,200. If the gross income is more than $1,800 and the net is $1,200 or more, the actual net earnings must be counted. The method makes it possible for many farmers to maintain their coverage under the program in years of little or no net earnings resulting from the sharp, and often uncontrollable, increases and decreases in earnings from the farm business.

As for agricultural laborers or farm workers, the wages earned count toward social security benefits if an employer pays the worker

$150 or more in cash during the year for farm work. In addition, if a worker does farm work for one employer for twenty or more days during a year for cash wages on a time basis such as an hour, day, or week, then his earnings count toward social security benefits even though less than $150. The purpose of these provisions for farm workers is to cover those who may work for a short period of time for many employers and also those who spend considerable time with a single employer but are paid at a very low rate. On the other hand, it is not intended to cover persons who are not substantially employed as farm workers, e.g., a schoolboy who may work three or four days during vacation.

The 1950 amendments also covered persons engaged in domestic service in the private home of the employer. Under present law such employment for a given employer is covered if such domestic worker was paid $50 or more in cash wages by that employer during a calendar quarter of three months.

Since 1939, most family employment has been excluded from coverage. A child under 21 in the employ of a parent, a parent in the employ of his son or daughter, or a husband or wife employed by the spouse, was not considered "employed" for social security purposes. The basis for this exclusion was the feeling that in family enterprises it would be difficult to tell whether or not an employer-employee relationship really existed. However, by 1960, these problems did not seem too great in certain cases of family employment and Congress extended coverage to parents who work in a trade or business for their sons or daughters. Domestic work performed by a parent in or about his child's private home or work not in the course of the child's trade or business still is not counted.

Beginning in 1957, persons in the uniformed services of the United States were covered in the same manner as employees in private industry, even though they are also covered by a liberal noncontributory pension plan. This includes all persons on active full-time duty with the armed services or reserves, annual training duty as reserve officers, or full-time duty as a commissioned officer in the Reserve Corps of the Public Health Service for training purposes. For practical purposes, all persons in uniform in the military services are covered. The Department of Defense or other government agency involved is treated the same as any other employer with reference to the tax and other requirements. Only base pay—and not allowances for dependents or the value of quarters and subsistence—counts for coverage purposes. Military service before 1957 is creditable on a "gratuitous" basis, with the cost of benefits paid by the general treasury, the credit allowed being equivalent to $160 per month.

United States citizens employed in the United States by foreign governments and international organizations are compulsorily covered on a self-employed basis (since their employer cannot be taxed). However, employment outside of the United States is generally excluded from coverage although under certain circumstances such employment may be covered. For example, an American citizen working abroad for an American employer is compulsorily covered, while American citizens working for an American corporation's foreign subsidiary may be covered by election on the part of the American corporation. Likewise, employees working on or in connection with an American vessel or aircraft are covered under certain conditions.

As previously stated, the Social Security Act originally covered only "employees" and excluded several million self-employed such as shop-owners, farmers, lawyers, dentists, physicians, and others. Today, practically all such persons are included pursuant to the 1950 amendments and subsequent enactments. The major group of self-employed still excluded are self-employed doctors of medicine.

Although coverage is generally compulsory, certain groups do have a choice as to whether they will be covered. Employees of nonprofit religious, charitable, educational, and certain other types of nonprofit organizations are not compulsorily covered. Such employees may be covered if the organization elects to be covered. Only those employees who elect coverage will be included in the initial coverage. However, once covered, continuation of coverage is compulsory, and coverage is likewise compulsory for all new employees. Ministers are excused from compulsory coverage on the theory of separation of Church and State; *i.e.*, the State did not wish to force such persons into the social security system. Such persons may elect to be covered as "self-employed." In general, they must make the election within two years of beginning such service or by April 15, 1962, whichever is later. If they so elect, they are covered in the same manner as self-employed persons and, upon election, coverage is thereafter compulsory.

In the United States approximately 6.5 million persons are employed by state and local governments. About three-quarters of these are covered by special retirement systems that these political subdivisions provide. Increasingly, however, these employees are also being covered by old-age, survivors, and disability insurance—about 60 per cent of those under these special systems are also under the old-age, survivors, and disability insurance system. In addition, about three-fifths of those not having such a special system are under old-age, survivors, and disability insurance, so that all but about 10 per cent have some retirement protection (and most of these 10 per cent are part-time employees, who may have retirement protection through another job or through a husband). Coverage of state and local government employees can be arranged by means of voluntary agreements entered into by the states with the Secretary of Health, Education, and Welfare.

Under the Social Security Act, the individual state may cover groups of state or local employees, who are not in positions covered under a state or local retirement system, at its discretion or that of its political subdivisions. With reference to employees already under a retirement system, in all states the agreement may cover all members of the retirement system under old-age, survivors, and disability insurance if a majority of the employees covered by such retirement plan vote to come under the OASDI system in a referendum held under authorization of the state.

Although coverage has become almost universal, reference has been made to those groups still excluded. Self-employed physicians have been excluded because the organized spokesman for physicians, the American Medical Association, has opposed such coverage. The American Medical Association's view is that other arrangements are more satisfactory for the physician. Many policemen and firemen are covered by local liberal pension programs which provide for early retirement (frequently after twenty years of service), and therefore have not desired coverage. Federal employees also have an excellent pension program and have not yet been able to accept a program which would integrate their retirement plan with old-age, survivors, and disability insurance.

Although only about six million of the nation's seventy million gainfully employed are ineligible for coverage, this lack of coverage constitutes "unfinished business."

The OASDI program has two aspects: it is both a tax on earnings and a benefit to specified groups. Many persons feel that no one who works should be excused from the payment of the tax. Likewise, the benefits should be available to all groups. Although coverage in the United States program is more widespread than in many countries with older systems, the minor gaps in coverage should be closed in order that the basic goal of the old-age, survivors, and disability insurance program may be achieved, namely, universal coverage. The opposition of groups, such as the self-employed physicians, to coverage should not be the guiding principle with reference to their inclusion any more than opposition to a general tax ought to exclude opponents thereof from the payment of the tax. Income security through social security is not only of benefit to the individual. It is a national goal and will be more fully achieved when all persons are covered. Every national administration and both industry and labor leaders have urged the achievement of this goal.

2. The Right to Benefits

Benefits are paid as a matter of "right." This is a fundamental element in the old-age, survivors, and disability insurance program. Benefits do not depend upon the discretion of administrators. The right to benefits is a statutory right which can be enforced by the courts.[75] Furthermore, it is a right which arises out of work and out of the payment of special taxes on the earnings from that work.

The rights of persons who have met the conditions detailed by the Social Security Act are protected by an appeals machinery. When benefits are denied or the individual is dissatisfied with the determination of the Social Security Administration, the claimant is entitled to several completely independent reviews of his case. He may first request the Social Security Administration to reconsider its original determination. Such a reconsideration constitutes an independent and thorough review of the case by an official who was not involved in the original decision. Usually, such request must be filed within six months from the date of notice of the initial determination. If still dissatisfied, the claimant may ask for a hearing before a hearing examiner of the Social Security Administration. These hearing examiners are well-trained lawyers or experts in social security law. They will hold hearings in or near the community in which the claimant resides. If they determine that an error has been made they may direct that the error be rectified. The claimant must file a request for such a hearing within six months after the date of notice of the reconsidered determination.

After a hearing and a decision by the hearing examiner, the claimant may request a review of the examiner's decision by the Appeals Council. Such request must be made within sixty days of the examiner's decision. The Appeals Council is an independent body, sitting as a quasi-judicial group, and its decisions are complied with by the Social Security Administration. If the claimant is still dissatisfied, he may bring a civil action in a United States District Court[76] within sixty days from the date of the Appeals Council decision.

3. Benefits

Benefits under OASDI provide protection against the risk of income loss resulting from old age, disability, and death. A person who has attained insured status may receive retirement benefits for himself and dependent's benefits for his spouse and children. Survivor benefits are paid, when the insured dies, to the surviving spouse, dependent parents, and children. A lump-sum payment is payable upon death of the insured worker to the surviving spouse if he or she lived in the same household; if there is no such spouse, it may go to pay for unpaid burial expenses, or to reimburse the person who paid the funeral expenses. For the insured person, disability benefits are available if the insured is too seriously disabled to work; dependent's benefits are then available for his wife and children.

These three basic benefits—old-age or retirement benefits, survivors benefits, and disability benefits—are administered as a single program.[77]

(a) Becoming Insured

As previously indicated, a person must be "insured" in order for social security benefits to be paid to him or his family. Being "insured" does not establish the *level* or *amount* of the benefit but merely eligibility for such benefit. The benefit amount is based on average earnings. Being "insured" involves earnings from "covered employment" for a sufficient number of "quarters of coverage."

A person obtains a quarter of coverage if, during a calendar quarter of three months, he has been paid $50 or more in wages in employment covered by law, other than for agricultural work and self-employment. If he is paid the maximum amount creditable and taxable ($4,800), he is credited with four quarters of coverage regardless of when the wages are paid. He also gets a quarter of coverage for each full $100 of wages from agricultural labor received in a calendar year (maximum of four quarters of coverage in a year).

A self-employed person must have covered net earnings of at least $400 during the year before any quarters are counted, and then he gets credit for four quarters of coverage.

All types of retirement and survivor benefits are generally payable if a person is *fully insured;* certain survivor benefits are also payable if the deceased is only *currently insured.* The requirements for the attainment of such status are quite detailed and complicated. For our purpose, the general rules will suffice.

Fully insured. A person who has forty quarters of coverage (ten years) is always fully insured. A person with less than forty quarters of coverage is nevertheless fully insured if he has been covered for at least one quarter for every year since 1950 and before age 65 for men and 62 for women, or prior to death; in all cases at least six quarters of coverage are required. The quarters of coverage may be acquired any time after 1936, including the period after age 65 (or 62).

An illustration will clarify this requirement. A man becomes 62 years of age in June 1964 and retires. He worked continuously as a self-employed store-owner from 1937 to 1955. If he had been a wage earner, he would have nineteen years of coverage or seventy-six quarters of coverage. However, such self-employed persons were first covered in 1951. A total of sixteen full calendar years elapsed after 1950 and up to the beginning of 1967, when he reaches age 65. To be fully insured at age 62 he must have at least sixteen quarters of coverage. He has twenty quarters for the five years, 1951 through 1955. Therefore, he is fully insured. In the case of a woman of similar employment history, only thirteen quarters of coverage (measured up to age 62) would be required.

Currently insured. A person is currently insured if he has at least six quarters of coverage during the thirteen-quarter period immediately preceding his death, disability, or retirement.

Insured status for disability benefits. To be eligible for disability benefits a worker, in addition to being disabled to the extent of being unable to do any substantial work, must have a total of twenty quarters of coverage out of the forty calendar quarters ending with the quarter in which he becomes disabled. He must also be fully insured.

The general purpose of the fully insured requirement is to establish long-term attachment to covered work as a basis for the benefits payable on account of old age. The general purpose of the currently insured requirement is to establish *recent* attachment to the labor market as a basis for benefits paid to young survivors. The general purpose of the disability insured status requirements is to establish recent substantial attachment, as well as long-term attachment, to covered work as a basis for the benefits payable on account of disability.

(b) Entitlement to Benefits

Workers and their dependents or survivors are entitled to a variety of benefits which cover the contingencies of retirement due to old age, disability, and death. Persons eligible to benefits are listed in Table I (Appendix). Benefits are not paid automatically. Persons who meet the requirements for a benefit must file an application for such benefit. If the application indicates that all of the legal requirements have been met, benefit payments will be awarded.

(c) Old-Age and Retirement Insurance Benefits

The largest of the programs under OASDI is that of old-age and retirement insurance benefits. Provision of benefits for retired workers was the basic program of social security from the beginning of the Social Security Act; benefits for dependents and survivors of workers were added in 1939. At the end of 1961, over thirteen mil lion persons age 62 or over were receiving old-age, survivors, and disability insurance benefits. In addition, many children of person who were in receipt of old-age retirement benefits were receiving dependents' benefits, and in such circumstance benefits were also paid to the wife of the retired worker regardless of her age.

Old-age insurance benefits are payable to a fully insured worke: who has reached the retirement age of 62, is fully insured, has ap plied for benefits, and has substantially retired. The minimum re tirement age of 62 for men was established by the 1961 amend ments, effective in August 1961, culminating twenty-five years of discussion as to the appropriate eligibility age for retirement bene fits (age 62 for women had been adopted in the 1956 amendments) Supplementary benefits are paid with respect to certain dependents of retired workers—the wife aged 62 or over; the dependent hus band aged 62 or over (actual recent dependency must be proved, and the wife must have been currently insured, as well as fully in sured); children under age 18, or regardless of age if disabled con tinuously since age 18 (for children of a woman worker, actual dependency must be proved, or she must have been currently in sured, as well as fully insured, at retirement); and wives regard less of age if an eligible child is in her care.

If a person is eligible for benefits on more than one earnings record (such as a woman with old-age benefits from her own work and wife's or widow's benefits), she gets only the larger of the benefits.

In 1956, Congress passed a provision to permit women to draw the wife's and old-age insurance benefits at age 62 but on a re duced basis. Widow's benefits and parent's benefits for a woman also became payable at age 62 at the full rate. Any reductions are permanent (*i.e.*, continue after age 65). The amount of the reduc tion for female retired workers is $5/9$ per cent for each month under age 65—*i.e.*, 20 per cent for retirement at exact age 62. The reduc tion for the wife's benefits is somewhat larger, $25/36$ per cent for each month (or a maximum reduction of 25 per cent for claiming benefits at exact age 62), since it is applicable only during the *joint* lifetimes of the husband and wife. For example, a woman worker eligible for a monthly benefit of $80 at age 65 received $64 at age 62, and a wife who would be entitled to a wife's benefit of $60 per month (one-half her husband's benefit) at age 65, would draw $45 per month if she retired at age 62. In 1961, Congress reduced the retirement age for men to 62 also. Like the women, men receive full retirement benefits if they retire at 65 but a reduced monthly payment if they become entitled before 65.

Over the years, the benefits have undergone substantial increases. In general, they have been raised to keep pace with the increased cost of living, although such benefit increases have been somewhat higher than such increased living costs but not high enough to keep pace with increasing wage levels.

All benefits are related to the "Primary Insurance Amount" (PIA) which is the amount paid to a retiring worker at or after age 65. Other benefit rates are calculated as a percentage of the insured person's primary insurance amount. The PIA is based on the "average monthly wage," figured as prescribed in the law. The average monthly wage is determined by taking the total earnings of the worker over a prescribed period of years and dividing by the number of months in that period. In determining total earnings, the law permits dropping out of consideration the lowest five years of earnings and also any period of disability. No earnings above the taxable earnings base (now $4,800, $4,200 in 1955–58, $3,600 in 1951–54, and $3,000 before 1951) are counted.

The benefit rate is determined from the average monthly wage by a benefit table in the law, which shows the PIA for every possible average monthly wage. This benefit table is based on a formula which is weighted in favor of persons with low average monthly earnings.

There are several alternative methods of computing the average wages for benefit purposes. The most common method, however, relates to work after 1950 and will suffice for our purposes here. Most persons working in covered employment have received their highest creditable earnings in and after 1951. This is due to the increases in the taxable earnings base over the years as well as the higher levels of employment and earnings during the past decade. In addition, many persons were not in covered employment prior to 1951 because the law excluded them from coverage. For covered earnings since 1950, the average wage is based on a number of years equal to all but five of the years elapsing after 1950 up to the year in which the worker attains age 65 (age 62 for women). Years before age 22 and years in established periods of disability are also not counted. Once the number of years is determined, the actual years used are those of highest earnings selected from all the years after 1950 up to or including the year in which the person applies for benefits (including years after age 65, or 62 for women, where retirement is delayed). The earnings for the years selected are averaged over the number of months in those years. The resultant average is translated to a benefit rate (PIA) by means of the table in the law. Where a person has additional earnings after his entitlement and qualifies for a recomputation of his benefit rate, years of higher earnings may be substituted for years previously used if the new average wage is higher.

For example, if a man attains age 65 in 1962, his average wage must be computed over his 6 highest years of earnings after 1950 (deducting 5 years from the 11 years after 1950 and before 1962). If he had earnings of $3,200 in each year in 1951–56, $3,800 in each year of 1957–59, $4,800 in each year of 1960–61, and $2,000 in 1962, then his 6 best years would be 2 years of $4,800, 3 years of $3,800, and 1 year of $3,200. The total earnings of $24,200 when divided by the 72 months in the 6 years yields an average monthly wage of $336 (rounded down to the whole dollar) and a benefit rate of $113 at age 65. If he continues to work after age 65 and has earnings of $4,000 in both 1963 and 1964, his average wage then will be based on 2 years at $4,800, 2 years at $4,000, and 2 years at $3,800, and so will be $350, yielding a benefit rate of $116.

If the man had attained age 62 in 1962 and retired then, his average wage would have to be computed over 9 years instead (deducting 5 years from the 14 years after 1950 and before 1965, when he will attain age 65). Under such circumstances, his best 9 years would be 2 years of $4,800, 3 years of $3,800, and 4 years of $3,200. His average monthly wage would be $312, and his primary insurance amount $108. (This amount would be reduced if paid before age 65.)

As can be seen, women are given an advantage over men in the computation of average monthly wage because the "termination point" for determining the measuring period is age 62 for them, rather than age 65. A woman reaching age 62 in 1962 with the same earnings record as for the man discussed above would have her average monthly wage based on only the 6 highest years after 1950, and so it would be $336 (as against $312 for a man born in the same year).

Minimum and Maximum Benefits. The minimum primary insurance amount is $40 per month (where the person takes an old-age benefit before age 65 his benefit will, of course, be reduced below $40); and the minimum monthly benefit for a family with more than one beneficiary is $60. The maximum monthly benefit is $127 for the PIA and $254 for the family.

Amounts payable for the different types of benefits and different average earnings are set forth in Table II in the Appendix. Benefits paid to families, survivors, and dependents are based on a percentage of the PIA subject to a maximum that is applicable when there are several beneficiaries drawing benefits on the same earnings record. This maximum, also determined by the benefit table in the law, is approximately 80 per cent of the average monthly wage, but never more than $254 (for average wages of $315 per month and over) or less than one and one-half times the PIA (for average wages of $127 and less). Benefits payable to the wife, child, or dependent husband or a retired or disabled insured worker are 50 per cent of the PIA; benefits paid to the widow, dependent widower, or dependent parent aged 62 or over are 82-1/2 per cent of the PIA (except that when two dependent parents are present, the rate is 75 per cent each); and each surviving child and the mother of a surviving child draw 75 per cent of the primary insurance amount. The benefits derived as a fraction of the primary insurance amount, as set forth above, are subject to reduction when paid to wives and dependent husbands first drawing benefits between 62 and 65, except that there is no reduction for the wife when an eligible child is present.

(d) Disability Insurance Benefits

Disability Insurance benefits have been added to the Social Security Act in recent years. Beginning in July 1957 benefits were paid to disabled workers between the ages of 50 and 65. Amendments in 1960 extended such benefits to disabled persons under age 50 if they meet the other requirements. The original age limitation (50 or over) was placed in the law in 1956 because of the alleged difficulty of predicting costs under this new feature. Subsequent experience indicated the limitation was unnecessary and today all persons who meet the requirements are eligible regardless of age. At the end of 1961, over 600,000 disabled workers were receiving benefits.

The benefit amounts payable in the event of disability are the same as those set forth previously for old-age benefits, and the methods of computing such benefits are the same. The benefit paid to the disabled beneficiary is the same amount he would receive if he were of retirement age at the time he became eligible for disability benefits. The benefits payable to the dependents of a disabled beneficiary are similar to dependent's benefits in the case of old-age insurance.

Two types of monthly disability benefits are provided: a disability insurance benefit payable to a fully insured disabled worker who has twenty quarters of social security coverage out of the forty-quarter period ending with the beginning of his disability; and a childhood disability benefit, payable to a dependent child of a retired, disabled, or deceased worker aged 18 or over where such child incurred the disability before becoming 18 and has been continuously disabled since that time. These benefits are payable to children of retired, disabled, or deceased insured workers.

In order to be eligible for disability benefits the worker must be so disabled that he is not able to engage in any substantial gainful activity. In addition, the impairment must have lasted at least six months and be expected to continue for a long and indefinite time. A worker need not be completely helpless or confined to his home. Inability to carry on his usual occupation, however, will not entitle the worker to benefits if he can do other substantial work.

Determinations of disability are made by state agencies—usually the state vocational rehabilitation agencies—by agreement with the Secretary of Health, Education, and Welfare. Under these agreements, state agencies act as the agents for the Federal Government and all expenses of these agencies that are incurred in the discharge of this function are paid for from the disability insurance trust fund. Although the Social Security Administration may reverse a state finding of disability, it may not reverse a state finding that no disability exists. A state disability determination may be revised to make it more favorable to the applicant only on appeal or court review.

In addition to the two types of cash benefits set forth above, there is a third type of protection. This protection involves "freezing" a disabled individual's insured status and earnings record to protect him against loss of future benefits or reduction in the amount of future benefits because of disability. It is similar to the "waiver of premium" in private insurance. In effect, it eliminates, in the computation of the average monthly wage, those months during which the worker was disabled. In general, the requirements of eligibility for this protection are similar to those for cash disability benefits. In certain cases of blindness, however, inability to do substantial work is not required. In addition to protecting the survivor and retirement benefit rights of workers entitled to disability benefits, the provision also protects future old-age and survivor benefit rights for a small group of workers who, for technical reasons, are not entitled to disability benefits.

(e) Survivors Insurance Benefits

The third type of benefits provided is that for survivors of the insured worker. If an insured worker dies, benefits can be paid to the surviving widow, dependent widower, dependent parent, or child of such deceased worker. Dependent widowers and parents must be at least age 62 (actual recent dependency must be proved, and for widower's benefits the deceased wife must have been both fully and currently insured). The widow must also be this age unless she is caring for an eligible child receiving benefits. Children of a woman worker must have been actually dependent on her, or she must have been currently insured. These survivor benefits are becoming increasingly important; at the end of 1962, almost three million young survivors and dependents were drawing benefits. The survivors' benefits are figured as a percentage of the deceased worker's primary insurance amount. As indicated previously, the widow aged 62 or over receives 82-1/2 per cent of the deceased husband's primary insurance amount, subject to the maximum family benefit provision. In that event, the widow will receive a proportionate reduction. The widower's insurance benefit is the same as that of the widow. The amount of the child's benefit as well as the mother's insurance benefit (while she is under age 62) is equal to 75 per cent of the deceased worker's primary insurance amount, subject to the family maximum benefit provisions. A parent's benefit is equal to 82-1/2 per cent of the primary insurance amount of the insured worker, but if both parents are entitled to receive benefits, then each receives only 75 per cent of the PIA. The lump-sum payment for death of an insured worker (including retired workers) is three times the PIA, but with a maximum of $255 (or in those cases, where only actual funeral expenses are reimbursed, such actual expenses, if less than the $255).

4. Contributory and Without Government Subsidy

The American system of old-age, survivors, and disability insurance has emphasized a principle not found in some of the social insurance programs of other countries. In contradistinction to some programs that are financed in part by general revenues of the government, the United States program is financed through contributions by employees, their employers, and the self-employed, without any subsidy from the general revenues of the government. Employers and employees each pay the same tax rate; the tax rate for a self-employed person is approximately one and one-half times the employee rate.

It is interesting that this principle of joint contributions by employer and employee was accepted in the original Social Security Act almost without debate.[78] The importance of the principle is that it encourages a responsible attitude on the part of those covered by the system. The taxpayer knows that the benefits for himself and his family are made possible by the payment of social security taxes, and this knowledge gives him a personal interest and stake in the soundness of the program. He realizes also that there is a relationship between the benefits received and the taxes that have been paid; he knows that increased benefits generally require increased taxes.

As a matter of pure economics, many students of the problem have maintained that it makes little difference whether the tax is solely on the employer or jointly shared. According to this view, it constitutes the same charge on industry and the cost of production. Although, as a matter of strict economics, this is true, the importance of the contributory principle arises from other factors. Any social security program is subject to change through legislative action. In the final analysis such legislative action in a democracy is dependent upon the voters. If the voters are contributors, as well as the ultimate decision makers with reference to social security, a more responsible attitude will be taken by both voters and their elected representatives with reference to social security programs. This has been demonstrated repeatedly in the hearings and debates before the committees of Congress. Representatives of organizations composed of large numbers of persons—labor groups, consumer groups, veterans' organizations, and others, for example, have consistently supported the principle that any new benefits should be financed by new taxes, that the system must be self-supporting, and that workers should bear part of the cost. The fact that almost every gainfully employed person makes contributions to the old-age, survivors, and disability insurance system has an important psychological aspect which has resulted in widespread support of the system. The individual is, at one and the same time, a voter, a contributor, and a prospective beneficiary. When the contributory principle is combined with other features of the system such as wage-related benefits, the protected groups can easily understand the direct relationship between benefits, earnings, and contributions; they feel greater psychological security in the protection afforded and at the same time the program is less susceptible to unsound changes by political pressure groups.[79]

This contributory principle, which was derived from the original German social insurance program, has been finding increasing support in nations which had earlier rejected this principle or adopted it only partially. For example, in Sweden it has been the subject of considerable discussion and has been accepted for part of the system. Canada, likewise, has been reviewing it; and in Great Britain a Royal Commission recently asserted that the contributory principle was "an important measure of social discipline." [80]

5. Financing

A major goal of the old-age, survivors, and disability insurance system is that it shall be soundly financed. Whether this goal has been achieved is a question upon which there is considerable difference of opinion. Nevertheless, the responsible committees of Congress have concluded that the financing basis of the program is sound. Likewise, the "major finding" of the Advisory Council on Social Security Financing in 1959 emphasized its financial soundness.[81]

The methods of financing and of the administration of the funds received and disbursed are set forth in the law. Employees and employers pay taxes in equal amounts on the first $4,800 of wages earned in a year from each employer. The tax rates are summarized in Figure 2, page 63. The self-employed pay taxes at a rate of approximately one and one-half times the rate paid by the employee. If a self-employed person also has covered wages in a year, he pays taxes on self-employment income only enough to bring his total wages and self-employment earnings up to $4,800. If an employee works for several employers during the course of a year, he pays taxes on earnings up to $4,800 from each employer (as do the employers) but receives a refund of taxes that he has paid on an aggregate of more than $4,800 of wages in the year (no refunds to his employers).

The taxes collected are placed in two trust funds—the Federal Old-Age and Survivors Insurance Trust Fund and the Federal Disability Insurance Trust Fund. The money in these funds not currently needed to pay benefits or administrative expenses is invested in United States Government securities and obligations and draws interest, which is added to the funds. The tax rates in the law plus the interest earned on the investments are intended to provide sufficient income to meet the anticipated expenditures for benefits and administrative costs into the indefinite future. Advisory

Councils on Social Security Financing periodically review the program and make recommendations as to its financial soundness.

As indicated, social security taxes are not paid on all earnings from the covered work; they are paid on earnings only up to $4,800 a year. A person earning $2,400, for example, pays one-half of the amount paid by a person earning $4,800, or more. Benefits likewise are based on average earnings.

Congress has raised the taxable wage base three times—from the original $3,000, to $3,600 in 1951, $4,200 in 1955, and $4,800 in 1959. Nevertheless, the percentage of income that is over the base and that remains untaxed is far greater than that prevailing in the early years of the program.

The point at which the maximum taxable earnings base should be set is the subject of considerable controversy. It assumes unusual importance for several reasons. Since benefits are earnings related, the higher the taxable income, the larger the benefit for the middle and higher income group. For example, when the base was raised from $4,200 (first effective in 1955) to $4,800 in 1959, the maximum benefit was thereby increased from $116 per month for a single worker, based on average yearly earnings of $4,200 to $127 per month for a single worker, based on average yearly earnings of $4,800.

A rise in the taxable earnings base increases the income to the fund. Since benefits are weighted for the low-income groups, the taxes on the higher earnings yield an income in excess of the outgo for the increased benefits. Under the law, a worker with high average earnings gets a monthly benefit that is a smaller percentage of his average monthly earnings than does a worker with low average earnings. For example, a man with average monthly earnings of $400 who begins to get benefits at or after age 65 will get a benefit of $127 a month, which is about a 32 per cent replacement of his average earnings; a man who had average monthly earnings of $100 and who begins to get benefits at or after age 65 will get a benefit of $59 a month, which is a 59 per cent replacement of his average earnings. On the other hand, taxes are a constant percentage of earnings. Therefore, increasing the earnings base results in a net increase in income to the program.

The point at which the earnings base is set affects an important philosophical and practical goal of the program. Most persons agree that the base should be raised from time to time. If benefits are to be raised to keep up with increased costs of living, the income to pay for such increases can come from increased taxes on the same earnings base or from increased income due to raising the base while retaining the same tax rate. In practice both the earnings base and the tax rates have increased over the years along with benefit increases. Those who believe that social security should provide only a "minimum floor of protection" and that higher-income groups should provide additional protection through their own efforts, generally oppose increases in the earnings base or urge minimal increases; those who believe that the program should provide benefits that increase as wages increase and thereby provide for the retired aged a share in the nation's increased productivity, urge greater increases in the earnings base. Furthermore, those who feel that earnings-related benefits are an important and valuable characteristic of the American program are concerned that the increase in the proportion of income not taxed, and therefore not credited toward benefits, will detract from the wage-related principle. For workers whose earnings exceed the maximum wage base, difference in earnings obviously do not result in differences in benefit amounts. If the wage base is not increased as wages go up, more and more of the workers of the country will have benefits at or very near the maximum, and old-age and survivors insurance will tend more and more toward a flat-benefit system. In such a case, the value of a wage-related system in providing security related to the individual's past living standards and in reinforcing incentives would be largely lost.

The tax rate is expressed as a percentage of the taxable income. The 1963 rate is 3-5/8 per cent for the employee up to $4,800 of wages. The employee earning $4,800 pays $174 per year; his employer pays the same amount. A self-employed person pays 5.4 per cent (one and one-half times the employee rate) or $259.20 per year. The tax rates will increase until they reach 4-5/8 per cent each for employers and employees and 6.9 per cent for self-employed in 1968. The tax rate is established so that the income from taxes and interest on the trust funds will keep the program in long-range actuarial balance over the indefinite future.

The tax rates in the past and those in the present law are as follows:

Figure 2

Contribution Rates Under Social Security Act
As of 1961

Year	Employee per cent	Employer per cent	Self-employment per cent
1937–1949	1	1	°
1950–1953	1-1/2	1-1/2	2-1/4 °
1954–1956	2	2	3
1957–1958	2-1/4	2-1/4	3-3/8
1959	2-1/2	2-1/2	3-3/4
1960–1961	3	3	4-1/2
1962	3-1/8	3-1/8	4-7/10
1963–1965	3-5/8	3-5/8	5-2/5
1966–1967	4-1/8	4-1/8	6-1/5
1968 and thereafter	4-5/8	4-5/8	6-9/10

° Not covered until 1951.

Of the taxes set forth above, 1/4 per cent of the tax on employees, 1/4 per cent of the tax on employers, and 3/8 per cent of the tax on self-employed are earmarked for the disability insurance program and the proceeds are placed in the Federal Disability Insurance Trust Fund; the remainder of the taxes are placed in the OASI Trust Fund. The benefits for disabled workers and their eligible dependents are paid from the Disability Insurance Trust Fund (and also the relevant administrative expenses). All other benefit payments and administrative expenses (including benefits for child-hood disability beneficiaries of retired and deceased workers) come out of the OASI Trust Fund. These tax rates for disability insurance are not expected to increase under the present provisions of the law since it is anticipated that they will be sufficient to finance the disability insurance program. The increases in the schedule are related to old-age and survivors insurance.

Basis for Estimating Future Costs. Since one objective in the financing of the old-age, survivors, and disability insurance program is to make it self-supporting, great care must be exercised in setting the tax rates in relation to benefits and administrative expenditures. The Division of the Actuary of the Social Security Administration is charged with the responsibility of making estimates which will accomplish this. Such estimates are extremely complicated. They involve assumptions relating to the number of employed, wage levels, average earnings, the rate of and average age of retirement, the incidence of death and disability, size of families (survivors), and a variety of other factors. These estimates are reviewed by Congressional committees and the Advisory Councils, who may recommend any needed adjustments in the tax rates. Adjustments in the tax rates have been made from time to time, as conditions changed and as changes were made in the program, in order to maintain the program on a sound financial or actuarial basis.

The concept of "actuarial soundness" has given rise to considerable confusion. The confusion arises over the attempt to apply the principles of "actuarial soundness" as practiced by life insurance companies and private pension plans to a social security program where the same principles are not applicable in their entirety.

Actuarial soundness in private insurance may be popularly expressed in this way: the insurance company should have sufficient reserves to pay off all of its contractual obligations in the event either that it goes out of business at the decree of its stockholders (or, if a mutual company, of its policyholders) by not accepting new policy applicants, or that all present policyholders decide to discontinue premium payments and take cash surrender value or other nonforfeiture options. In a government-sponsored social security program, the financing is based on the assumption that the program will continue indefinitely and that there will always be new entrants. It is unnecessary, then, to build up reserves on the premise that the sponsoring body, the government, will terminate its activities. In a government social security program, therefore, the test of actuarial soundness is not tied completely to the size of the reserves but is related to the question of whether anticipated income will always be sufficient over a long-range period to pay the anticipated expenditures. The "reserve" under such a system can be of any size provided it is large enough to cover those few years when expenditures may exceed income.

Judged by this principle of "financial soundness," the social security program is "actuarially sound" and has been so characterized by Congressional committees and students of the problem.[82]

The two trust funds serve two primary purposes: They produce income from the investment in government securities and thus help defray some of the costs of the program; and they constitute contingency reserves which can be used in those years when expenditures exceed income. Under present estimates, it is expected that the trust funds, totalling more than $22 billion at the end of 1961, will continue to grow and remain large enough to take care of foreseeable contingencies. Under present estimates, and the tax rates now in the law, the OASI Trust Fund is expected to continue to increase every year after 1963 for at least the next twenty years. The Disability Insurance Trust Fund is expected to grow for the next ten years and then decrease gradually. The status of these funds will, of course, be affected by any program changes that may be made by the Congress.

The trust funds are kept completely separate and apart from other funds in the General Treasury. A certain amount is kept in cash, sufficient to take care of the current cash expenditures; the remainder is invested in government securities which, in general, draw the same rate of interest as long-term government securities that are being sold in the open market at the time of such purchase. Although some persons have questioned the use of the trust funds for the purchase of government securities, it appears to be the only practical method of handling such huge reserves. The alternative methods of managing these funds are limited and do not appear to be practical or desirable: they could be invested in private securities or private businesses; they could be collected and stored and not put to any special use; they could be invested in public projects such as public housing; or they could be invested in state or local government securities.

All of these alternatives have been considered from time to time, but the studies have always resulted in the conclusion reached by the 1959 Advisory Council which recommended that:

investment of the trust funds should, as in the past, be restricted to obligations of the United States Government. Departure from this principle would put trust fund operations into direct involvement in the operation of the private economy or the affairs of State and local governments. Investment in private business corporations could have unfortunate consequences for the social security system—both financial and political—and would constitute an unnecessary interference with our free enterprise economy. Similarly, investment in the securities of State and local governments would unnecessarily involve the trust funds in affairs which are entirely apart from the social security system.

The Trust Funds are managed by a Board of Trustees, which by law consists of the Secretary of the Treasury, the Secretary of Labor, and the Secretary of Health, Education, and Welfare. The Commissioner of Social Security serves as Secretary of the Board of Trustees. The Secretary of the Treasury is the "Managing Trustee" and is charged with the responsibility of investing and disbursing the funds. The Board issues an annual report on the status of the Funds.

The concern of Congress regarding social security financing and its desire to assure financing on a sound basis led to an amendment to the Social Security Act in 1956 establishing a series of Advisory Councils on Social Security Financing. These councils are established for the purpose of "reviewing the status of the Federal Old-Age and Survivors Insurance Trust Fund and of the Federal Disability Insurance Trust Fund in relation to the long-term commitments of the old-age, survivors, and disability insurance programs." The first such council completed its work on January 1, 1959.

The next council must be appointed by the Secretary of Health, Education, and Welfare in 1963 and is to consist of the Commissioner of Social Security as chairman and twelve other members. The members, under the law, must "to the extent possible, represent employers and employees in equal numbers, and self-employed persons and the public." It must report its findings not later than January 1, 1965, a year preceding the tax increase scheduled for 1966, and such findings are submitted to Congress in the report of the Board of Trustees. This particular council will also study the over-all status of the program—as to coverage, benefit adequacy, and all other aspects. Subsequent councils—to deal only with financing aspects—are to be appointed in 1966 and every fifth year thereafter and are to report in the same manner.

6. Compulsory

Another feature of the system is that coverage is compulsory, with very few exceptions. This principle has been adhered to since the beginning of the system, in order to protect it from adverse selection of risks as well as to protect the country as a whole against widespread destitution due to the very risks insured against, namely, old age, disability, and death of the wage earner.

The 1950 and subsequent amendments, which provided for elective coverage for some categories, did not represent a reversal in the intent of Congress to preserve the compulsory character of the system. On occasions when voluntary coverage on an individual basis (such as for farmers) was proposed, Congress has recognized that this involved grave dangers with respect to the financing of the system—those most likely to elect coverage would be persons who could expect the largest return for a relatively small contribution. Furthermore, persons who could most easily spare the money, rather than those who most needed the protection, would be more likely to elect to participate. Overriding considerations of a special character, however, entered into the decisions to introduce certain voluntary elements into the coverage. Constitutional barriers generally preclude the Federal Government from imposing the employer tax upon state and local governments and, traditionally, certain nonprofit institutions have been tax-exempt. These groups were therefore brought into coverage on a limited elective basis. Because, generally speaking, coverage is not optional for individual employees of states or localities or of nonprofit institutions, but rather is on a group basis—with new employees compulsorily covered—it does not involve the financial risk to the system inherent in an individual election.

In providing coverage for ministers through individual election, in the 1954 amendments, the Committee on Finance of the Senate stated:

A provision for coverage on an individual election basis, while not generally desirable, is considered by your committee to be justified in this area because of the special circumstances. Many churches have expressed the fear that their participation in the old-age and survivors insurance program as employers of ministers might interfere with the well-established principle of separation of church and state. Many church representatives also believe that individual ministers who do not wish to be covered on grounds of conscience should not be required to participate in the program.

Significantly, although proposals for coverage on an individual election basis have been made over the years in connection with several other groups—such as farm operators and self-employed professional persons—clergymen have been the only group for which this basis of coverage has been acceptable to Congress. Even then strict provisions as to coverage are included—a limited period to make election and then irrevocability of election once made.

7. Wage-Related

Again in contradistinction to some social insurance systems, the social security program in the United States emphasizes the relation of the economic status of the worker to the benefits he receives.[83] This accords with a firmly ingrained belief on the part of the American people that a man should receive rewards in accordance with his individual efforts and contributions.

Furthermore, the wage-related principle makes it possible to pay retirement incomes that are related to differing individual levels of living and to diverse economic conditions in different parts of the country. By and large, a person's earnings from work establish his level of living and determine the income he will want to maintain in retirement. If benefits were provided in the same amount for everyone, the amount would have to be either so high for some that it would exceed their earnings, or it would be so low for those who had worked at higher earnings levels that it would not provide meaningful security for them. Many countries which previously rejected the wage-related principle have adopted it or are now considering the advisability of adopting it.

8. Family-Oriented

Increasingly, the old-age, survivors, and disability insurance program has been changed to bring protection to members of the family of the insured. Upon the death, retirement, or disability of a worker, the family income may cease completely or become substantially lowered. Many children are in homes where family income has been insufficient to build up substantial personal financial reserves or where there is not sufficient life insurance to maintain the family over an extended period of time. In many families with young children, the father has not yet reached his full earning power and the mother is needed at home to care for the children. During such a period, the parents have had to meet the extra expenses of setting up the home and starting the family, so they often have not been able to save much money. In our culture, great emphasis has been placed on the importance of maintaining the family intact, and the maintenance of income becomes an important tool in the furtherance of this goal.

For these reasons, it is important that families with children have some assured means of support when the breadwinner's earnings stop or are greatly reduced. Survivors' insurance benefits for surviving children and their mothers constitute over half of the survivor benefits protection under the old-age, survivors, and disability insurance system. Protection is also provided for wives and children of disabled workers, for aged spouses of retired workers, and for aged spouses and parents of deceased workers. As previously explained, benefits extend to parents, wives or husbands, and widows or widowers, as well as to children. Because of the survivor protection afforded by old-age, survivors, and disability insurance, nine out of ten mothers and young children in the nation now have the assurance that they can receive monthly benefits if the father of the family dies.

Although survivor benefits were not provided in the original 1935 Act, they were included in 1939 even before old-age retirement benefit payments started. Additional categories of dependents were added in subsequent amendments. At the end of 1961, 3.8 million persons received such survivor benefits, and an additional 3.1

million persons received benefits as dependents of old age and disability retirants. The importance of the survivors' aspect of social security may be gleaned from the following table:

Figure 3

OASDI Survivor and Dependents' Benefits as of December, 1961

Category of Dependent	Number Receiving (in thousands)	Monthly Rate of Expenditures (in millions)
Survivor children*	1,650	$ 87.0
Children of retired workers *	338	8.5
Children of disabled workers *	291	8.5
Mothers of survivor children receiving benefits	428	25.4
Widows and widowers	1,697	110.2
Wives and husbands of retired workers	2,392	94.4
Wives and husbands of disabled workers	118	3.9
Parents of deceased workers	37	2.5

* Included among the child beneficiaries are about 123,000 disabled children aged 18 or over who have been disabled since before attaining age 18 (52,000 survivor children, 65,000 children of old-age beneficiaries, and 6,000 children of disability beneficiaries).

9. Replacement of Lost Earnings

A basic principle of the old-age, survivors, and disability insurance system is that benefits are paid only when earnings cease or become lower because of one of the three risks which are "insured," namely, old age or retirement, death, or disability. Old-age, survivors, and disability insurance is not generally an annuity system or pension program based upon age, disability, or death alone. Benefits are not generally paid to persons who have suffered no loss of income. This concept is an extremely important one but has given rise to one of the most controversial features in the program, namely, the "work test" or "retirement test." [84]

Simply stated, the retirement test provides a method of determining whether a worker has "retired" from gainful employment as required by law. Since the risk insured against is *loss* of earned income from work due to old age, retirement, or death of the breadwinner, the retirement test establishes a standard to ascertain whether the situation of the worker and his family is such as to warrant the conclusion that the contingency insured against, namely, loss of earned income, has occurred.

Under the present law, a worker who is 72 years of age or over is considered retired regardless of earnings. This recognizes the practical situation that very few persons over age 72 are actively working. Also, without the age-72 provision, people who worked to a very advanced age might never get benefits even though they had paid contributions longer than most other people. When a worker applies for benefits after age 62 and before reaching age 72, the retirement test applies, and it applies to earnings from all types of employment, not merely covered employment. A worker may receive full benefits if he earns $1,200 or less in a year. In general, if he earns above $1,200, then his benefits may be decreased by $1 for every $2 earned up to $1,700, i.e., on the next $500 of earnings over and above the $1,200. For all earnings above $1,700, $1 of benefits may be withheld for each dollar earned.

The above-described provisions, it is important to note, are only one part of the retirement test, namely, the yearly portion. Even though the yearly test might call for withholding of a certain amount of benefits, such amount might not be withheld, depending upon the monthly work record. The monthly part of the test provides that in no case shall benefits be withheld for any month in which the beneficiary has *wages* of $100 or less *and* does not render substantial services in self-employment. (The effect of earnings in reducing benefits is set forth in Table III in the Appendix.)

The retirement test applies to all types of beneficiaries except disability beneficiaries (both disabled workers and child disability cases). In respect to the latter category, any significant earnings would raise the question as to the continued existence of the disability. Any withholding of benefits in respect to the earnings of the retired worker is applicable not only to his own benefit but also to those of his dependents who are receiving benefits based on his earnings record. When a person receiving dependents' or survivor benefits has earnings sufficient to be affected by the retirement test, withholding will occur but only against his own benefits and not against those of other family members. For example, in a survivor-benefit case, the widowed mother might work sufficiently to have all her benefits withheld, but this will not affect the benefits of the children.

Although controversial, the retirement test supports a basic concept of the program, namely, that the risk insured against is not just old age or death but *loss* of earned income due to these factors. To abolish the test would change the character of the program from insurance against earnings loss to an annuity program under which persons who continued to work full time at their regular jobs could receive full benefits at age 65. There were at the end of 1961 about thirteen million persons who could qualify for retirement benefits; *i.e.*, they have been in covered employment long enough to be insured for retirement benefits, or the person on whose earnings record they could draw benefits has been so employed. Of these thirteen million, about one and one-half million were not getting benefits presumably because they (or the persons on whose earnings records they could draw benefits) were still working. These one and one-half million persons would receive benefits if an "annuity" arrangement were provided. To abolish the test would require an increase in the combined employer-employee tax rate of almost 1 per cent of covered earnings in order to keep the program self-supporting. The tax would be paid by all workers and their employers for the benefit of persons beyond retirement age who have substantial income. Whenever the retirement test provision has been examined by Congressional or other official groups, it has usually been concluded that the test, in some form, should be retained and that the contributions made by all gainfully employed should be used to pay benefits to persons most in need of them because of lack of earnings rather than as an addition to earnings for those who have not substantially retired.

Undoubtedly, the retirement test will be the subject of considerable discussion; it will probably be changed from time to time; it appears, however, destined to remain a basic concept of the old-age, survivors, and disability insurance program for some time to come.

10. Federal Administration

The old-age, survivors, and disability insurance program is one of the largest administrative operations of the Federal Government.

The Social Security Administration alone has more than 33,000 employees engaged in the maintenance of earnings records for all America's covered workers—involving about 112 million separate accounts of persons living at the end of 1962 who have had some covered earnings; a payment monthly to eighteen million beneficiaries (at the end of 1962) in the United States and more than one hundred other countries; and paying out in benefits over one billion dollars a month. Additional functions related to the program are performed by the Internal Revenue Service, which collects the social security taxes; the Disbursing Office of the Department of the Treasury, which prepares and mails the benefit checks; and the Secretary of the Treasury, who is the managing trustee of the Trust Funds. This entire operation is conducted at a cost of approximately 2 per cent of the social security taxes received and is generally regarded as one of the best and most efficiently operated programs of the Federal Government.

The Social Security Administration is headed by a Commissioner of Social Security, appointed by the President. The Secretary of Health, Education, and Welfare has delegated the basic operating functions of the programs of the Social Security Administration to the Commissioner, who supervises and directs the old-age, survivors, and disability insurance programs previously described. In addition, he also supervises the Bureau of Federal Credit Unions. This Bureau charters organizations which promote savings on the part of members by accepting deposits and making low-interest loans to such members.

Under the Commissioner of Social Security, the basic operating programs of old-age insurance, survivors insurance, and disability insurance are conducted from the headquarters offices in Baltimore, Maryland. It is here that all of the earnings records are kept through a completely mechanized and electronic filing and computing system which makes it possible to examine all of the 140 million earnings records (including those in respect to deceased persons and those with no recorded earnings) in eight to nine hours. Approximately six hundred district offices of the Social Security Administration are scattered throughout the country. In addition, there are 3,600 contact stations where Social Security representatives are available on a part-time basis. In these district offices account numbers are issued, claims for benefits are taken and developed, information is disseminated to the public, and incorrect or incomplete reports of workers' earnings are straightened out. In addition to these offices, travelling representatives serve the small towns and rural areas so as to minimize travel on the part of the public.

The basic laws governing the program are contained in the Social Security Act as amended and in certain related laws passed by the Congress.[85] These laws are put into effect by the Bureau pursuant to "Regulations" promulgated by the Commissioner of Social Security, with the approval of the Secretary of Health, Education, and Welfare.[86] These laws and regulations are available to the public.

All persons working in covered employment are required to procure a social security card. This card is secured by applying to the nearest district office. The card carries a social security account number, which remains the account number of the individual for life, and distinguishes the record of his earnings from those of others.

Social security taxes of employees are deducted from their pay. Every three months, the employer files a report of these deductions, adds his own equal social security contributions, and forwards the report and money to the United States Treasury. Large employers must make advance deposits of contributions monthly. In the case of employers of agricultural workers, the reporting is on an annual basis. From the Treasury Department, the records are transferred to the Bureau, and the earnings on which taxes were paid are credited to the worker's individual account. Receipts for the deducted social security taxes are given to the employee by the employer at least annually or possibly earlier if the worker's employment is terminated. The worker may obtain information as to the status of his account at any time by making inquiry on a form provided for that purpose and obtainable at any of the district offices. A self-employed person pays his social security tax annually after the close of the year along with his Federal income tax.

When a worker becomes eligible for benefits, in order to receive them he must file a claim. District offices assist workers in preparing such claim, but the claimant is responsible for submitting all necessay evidence as to age, disability, or other data. The district office then requests a copy of the earnings record from Baltimore and makes a preliminary decision as to whether the claim (other than for disability benefits) has been established, and, if so, the amount of the benefit. It then forwards the entire file to one of the seven payment centers, for review and final decision. The payment center, if it approves the claim, requests the appropriate office of the United States Treasury to draw the check and the claimant receives his monthly benefit through the mail on the third of every month or within a day or two thereafter.

A fundamental feature of the old-age, survivors, and disability insurance program is that the records kept by the Bureau are confidential. Information which is essential for the worker's record is not available except for purposes connected with the program or for other very limited purposes established by law. The worker is thus assured that the files will not be available to persons, organizations, or even government agencies except as clearly established by law and regulation.

The old-age, survivors, and disability insurance program in the United States is a growing and evolving program, and changes and improvements are being made in the program at almost every session of Congress. It has, it is true, some gaps and inadequacies, some of which have been touched upon.[87] On the other hand, it has emerged in twenty-seven years as the largest social insurance program in the world, bringing financial benefits every month to eighteen million aged, disabled, survivors, and dependents; it has become a large and important institution in the United States with widespread support throughout the population. Unquestionably, its provisions will be subject to discussion and change for many years to come but it constitutes a sound program to insure the American people against the risk of loss of income due to old age, death, or disability.

"Social security is a major feature of public social policy today. From tentative beginnings in a few countries in the early decades of the present century, it has rapidly become a big factor in the lives of many millions of people throughout the world." [88]
—*J. Henry Richardson*

CHAPTER VI

Unemployment Insurance

In every society, and under every economic system, there are periods when individual workers are unable to engage in gainful employment even though able and willing to work. This is especially true in an industrial society where most workers depend upon employment by a business or industrial enterprise. Persons may be involuntarily unemployed for many reasons: seasonal, cyclical, technological, or geographical unemployment (*i.e.*, unemployment in a particular area due to local conditions), and a variety of other causes. Although there are many ways of classifying the principal types of unemployment, in general it may be said that unemployment is of five types.

First, there is mass unemployment due to basic economic difficulties such as those responsible for the Great Depression of the 1930's.

Second, there is individual unemployment due to physical or mental disability, sickness, lack of work skills, or other reasons associated with personal situations.

Third, there is "frictional" unemployment generally associated with localized situations such as business failure, fire, flood, or stoppage of necessary supplies.

Fourth, there is seasonal unemployment which is characteristic of certain industries such as agriculture or fishing. Seasonal unemployment may also be due to weather conditions.

Fifth, there is technological unemployment. There are two types. The first involves shifts in consumption, production, or other patterns such as shifts from coal to oil for heating or from cotton or wool to synthetic fibers. The second involves automation and mechanization, which are making many skills obsolete and greatly reducing the need for unskilled labor.

Efforts to alleviate the social and economic effects of unemployment have taken many forms in the past—private charity, public relief, public work programs, union benefit funds—all these and more have been tried by industrial nations.

Today, in the United States, as well as in other countries, efforts to tackle the unemployment problem divide into programs to maintain full employment and programs to alleviate the effects of unemployment. The former include various methods, such as government subsidies to bolster specific parts of the economy and engaging in public works. With reference to the latter, many industrial nations including the United States have developed systems of unemployment insurance. Unemployment insurance is a program designed to partially replace income lost by reason of unemployment through the payment to unemployed workers of a specific amount of money for a limited period of time. It is particularly effective in cases of seasonal unemployment because it provides cash income during the temporary unemployment. With reference to mass unemployment due to economic conditions or technological unemployment, such unemployment insurance provides a first line of defense against the stoppage of income; it absorbs a substantial share of the initial impact of unemployment on the economy and provides immediate assistance to the individual for a time during which other measures can be designed to meet the particular problem. Unemployment insurance schemes are less common than other social insurance programs, even in the industrialized countries. Whereas in 1958, 77 countries had workmen's compensation programs (for industrial injuries and diseases), 58 had old-age insurance or old-age pension programs, and 59 had health insurance programs, only 26 had unemployment insurance programs.[89] The failure of many countries to include unemployment insurance as part of their social insurance program is attributable to several factors. Many have put more emphasis on public works or rigidly controlled labor markets, and some nations have such a small number of workers regularly employed for wages by others that unemployment insurance has not appeared practical. Unemployment insurance is designed primarily for an industrial wage economy and is not as easily adapted to an agricultural economy. In a few nations, employers carry the responsibility for maintaining their work force even when no work is available.

Unemployment insurance evolved from out-of-work benefit funds maintained by labor unions and mutual benefit societies during the nineteenth century in Europe. In the latter part of the century local governments began to subsidize such labor union funds. These initial efforts were sporadic and poorly financed; they failed to cover workers who were not members of the trade unions, and in general they were inadequate to meet the recurring unemployment crises. In 1789, the first public program was established by Basel Town in Switzerland but it lasted only a few years. It was not until 1893 that Berne, Switzerland, took the next step in the evolution of unemployment insurance, namely, government subsidies to voluntary plans covering nonunion workers. Other cities began subsidizing the unemployment funds of trade unions. It was not until 1911 that Great Britain established an unemployment insurance program which, although very limited, was the first nation-wide program.

In spite of the lack of legislation in the United States, interest in unemployment insurance had been growing since the turn of the century. As unemployment mounted after 1930, states began consideration of unemployment insurance as an answer to the widespread hardship which ensued. Only Wisconsin (in 1932) established such a system prior to the Social Security Act.[90]

In the meantime, unemployment insurance had become a national political issue. The Democratic Party platform of 1932 stated, "We advocate unemployment and old-age insurance under state laws." As unemployment mounted and suffering increased, the pressure for unemployment insurance grew.

UNEMPLOYMENT INSURANCE UNDER THE SOCIAL SECURITY ACT

The Committee on Economic Security generally favored a Federally operated and administered program of unemployment insurance similar to those of Germany and Great Britain. However, President Roosevelt preferred a state-operated program, and this became the recommendation of the Committee. The program today is similar to that in the original Social Security Act.

Unemployment insurance is primarily a state-administered program. The Social Security Act provides incentives to the individual states to establish state programs which meet certain standards and conditions. The Federal law provides a tax on employers in industry and commerce who employ four or more persons for at least twenty weeks of the year. Such employers pay a tax of 3.1 per cent on the first $3,000 of annual wages of an employee.[91] However, if a state establishes a program which is approved under the Federal law (Federal Unemployment Tax Act), employers in that state receive an offset of 2.7 per cent of the 3.1 per cent Federal tax. This Federal tax removed the original obstacles to state action. Prior to the Social Security Act, employers opposed state action on the ground that it would put them at a disadvantage in relation to employers in other states because such employers in other states would not have to pay the increased taxes.

All of the states (as well as Puerto Rico and the District of Columbia) have unemployment insurance programs approved under the Social Security Act and the Federal Unemployment Tax Act. Employers who are subject to these laws pay their state tax, and receive credit against their Federal tax. The remaining Federal tax—0.4 per cent of covered payroll—is collected by the Federal Government and is used to cover the cost of Federal administration, state administration (including the operation of public employment offices) and, since 1954, to bolster the reserves of state programs. There is a separate unemployment insurance system for railroad workers. Federal Government employees are covered under the state systems, with the Federal Government paying the full cost of the benefits actually paid. Similarly, coverage is provided on a special basis for those leaving military service.

Since unemployment insurance is a state program, there is wide variation among the states with reference to specific provisions. In general, the unemployment insurance program in the United States may be summarized as follows: the Federal Government imposes a tax on all industrial and commercial employers of four or more; if the state levies taxes to support an approved state plan, such state taxes are credited against a portion of the Federal tax; each state is free to establish its own program if it complies with certain Federal requirements; the portion of the tax (0.4 per cent) which is remitted to the Federal Government is placed in the general revenues, and Congress annually appropriates it for the purpose already mentioned. The state taxes are placed in state reserve funds in the Federal Treasury. From these funds, the states make weekly payments to unemployed persons for periods generally ranging from 26 to 39 weeks in varying amounts averaging $34 or more per week (April 1962).

The Bureau of Employment Security in the United States Department of Labor is the Federal agency charged with responsibility for the Federal Government's part in the program. It determines whether the state program meets Federal requirements and determines the amount of Federal grants to the states for administration. Each state has an "employment security agency" which administers the program. Generally, the same agency which administers the public employment offices handles claims for benefits as well as acting as employment exchanges to place people in available jobs. There are 1,800 local offices of these state employment agencies and they constitute a nation-wide system of public employment offices affiliated with the United States Employment Service, which is part of the Bureau of Employment Security. These state employment agencies actually preceded the Social Security Act. In 1933, Congress established a Federal-state system of employment offices, and since 1941 the Federal Government provides complete financing of these state employment offices.

Although state plans vary, all of them must meet certain minimum Federal requirements. Each state must deposit the unemployment insurance taxes it collects in the United States Treasury. The Treasury keeps a separate account for each state from which account the state may withdraw funds to pay unemployment benefits. The state must establish such methods of administration as will assure the full payment of benefits when due. Although benefits may be denied if a worker refuses to accept appropriate employment, benefits cannot be withheld if he refuses to accept a job under certain conditions designed to protect standards of prevailing wages, working conditions, and union affiliation. When a worker is unemployed, he reports to the local employment office. If the local employment office cannot place such worker in a suitable job, the worker may file a claim for unemployment benefits. Such benefits are paid to the worker, usually weekly, in an amount and for a period determined by state law. Generally, the amount is about 50 per cent of past earnings, subject to a maximum.

Subject to these Federal requirements, the states have great latitude in deciding who shall be covered, the amount and duration of benefits, the taxes to be paid, and procedures for handling claims.

GENERAL PATTERN OF STATE UNEMPLOYMENT INSURANCE LAWS

Unemployment insurance differs from state to state and only the general pattern can be set forth herein. The general characteristics of these state programs emerge as we review them under the four headings of coverage, eligibility for benefits, benefit payments, and financing.

Coverage

Workers covered by the system generally include all employees in private industry and commerce such as workers in factories, stores, mines, and offices, and Federal Government employees. In contradistinction to old-age, survivors, and disability insurance, which covers almost all workers, unemployment insurance varies in coverage from state to state. Generally excluded are agricultural and domestic workers, certain casual labor, employees in some governmental and nonprofit agencies, and employees in firms of less than four workers. On the average in 1960, about 45.6 million employees were covered by the Federal-state program of unemployment insurance with an additional 0.9 million covered by the railroad unemployment insurance system. Approximately 13.9 million employees still remain uncovered. Exclusions are due to the fact that most of the states have not included employment except that covered by Federal law, and Federal law covers only certain types of employment, and those only in firms employing four or more. In most states, workers excluded from Federal requirements may be covered upon the voluntary election of the employer.

Agricultural labor is generally excluded, accounting for approximately 1.9 million of the uncovered workers. Approximately two and one-half million domestic servants are excluded from coverage. Only New York and Hawaii cover domestics employed in private homes. All states exclude employment of a parent by his or her child, employment of a child under 21 years of age by a parent, or employment by a spouse. The basis for these exclusions is the difficulty of determining whether an employment relationship does, in fact, exist or when true unemployment begins.

The Federal Act does not cover employees of state and local governments because of the prohibition in the Constitution with reference to Federal taxation of state governments and their local subdivisions. As a result, approximately 5.6 million state and local government employees are not covered. However, thirty states provide some type of coverage. In some states the coverage extends to most employees; in others, coverage is limited. Likewise, approximately 1.7 million workers in nonprofit organizations which conduct charitable, educational, religious, or related programs are generally excluded.

Although the old-age, survivors, and disability insurance system now covers the self-employed (except for doctors), unemployment insurance does not. Unemployment insurance in the United States has developed as a system of insurance against wage loss due to unemployment and is, therefore, appropriately applied primarily to those who work for wages. In addition, it is extremely difficult to determine when a self-employed person is unemployed. California has been experimenting with a limited coverage of the self-employed. In that state, a self-employed person may elect coverage and if the state approves such coverage, the self-employed person pays taxes on $250 a month of earnings, which is assumed to be his earnings for purposes of coverage.

A group of employees of small firms (approximately 1.7 million) are not covered. The original Act applied only to firms of eight or more employees. In 1954, the Social Security Act was amended so that beginning in 1956 all employees in firms of four or more who worked at least one day a week for twenty weeks a year would be covered, and twenty-four states cover some firms with less than four employees.

The size of the firm is not the only consideration. Some state require a minimum payroll, other states (thirty-five) require variou periods of employment. The trend is definitely toward liberalizing these provisions, and there is now a growing conviction upon the part of those who have studied the problem that there should be no "size of firm" restriction and that all employers of one employee o more should be covered by Federal law.

Eligibility for Benefits

Although the states have certain general patterns of coverage because of the provisions of the Federal law, the states have great variation in eligibility for benefits and benefit amounts, since each state is free to determine the eligibility requirements and benefit amounts of unemployed workers.

In general, a person to be eligible for unemployment insurance benefits must be unemployed, able and available for work, and actively seeking such work. In addition, he must not (1) have left his job voluntarily, (2) have been discharged for misconduct, (3) be unemployed because of a strike, lockout, or other labor dispute or (4) have refused an offer of suitable employment. In addition to the general requirements mentioned above regarding a worker' unemployment, ability to work, and availability for work, there are a number of other eligibility requirements.

To be eligible for benefits, a worker must show that he wa employed in covered employment for the required length of time during a period called the "base period," or have earned a minimum amount in that period, or both. There is considerable state variation Forty-five states have a waiting period of one week during which the unemployed person receives no benefits. All persons seeking unemployment insurance must register for work at a public employment office. Benefits are not granted automatically upon unemployment. The worker must file a claim for such benefits, and the benefits are based on such claim being approved.

A worker may be disqualified from receiving benefits for a variety of reasons. Although disqualification provisions vary, generally a worker is disqualified if he refuses to register for work or accept suitable employment, leaves a job voluntarily without good cause, is not making reasonable efforts to obtain suitable employment, or is nemployed due to a labor dispute. This last requirement has been ncluded so that unemployment insurance will not become involved n taking sides in a labor-employer controversy. Disqualification usually results in delaying receipt of benefits; in only a few states loes it result in terminating or reducing benefits. Usually, the disqualification is for a specific number of weeks. The general theory or the limitation to a specific number of weeks is that, if the worker emains unemployed after the disqualification and is thereafter able und willing to accept suitable employment, his continued unemployment is more likely to be due to the lack of available jobs than to the original disqualifying act.

Benefit Payments

Benefits vary widely from state to state, and the Social Security Act does not set up any required standards. The weekly benefit amount, the duration of benefits, dependents benefits, and other benefit factors show great differentials. Benefits are paid on a weekly basis, and all states except New York determine "unemployment"as meaning a week of unemployment. New York pays benefits on the basis of days of unemployment.

In general, benefits are wage-related with minimum and maximum benefits set by state law; they are aimed at giving the worker a benefit equal to approximately 50 per cent of his weekly wage, subject to a maximum which in some states is so low that the 50 per cent goal cannot be reached; they are given to the worker for a maximum number of weeks which now is twenty-six weeks or more in most states.

Thirty-nine states base benefits on the highest aggregate wages earned in any quarter during the base period. Some states then take a fraction of these wages as the benefit. For example, in ten states the fraction is 1/26. In such states the following would be the result:

Assume employment for the full 13 weeks of the quarter at $50 per week. One twenty-sixth of the total wages of $650 (*i.e.,* 13 times $50) yields a benefit of $25 per week—50 per cent of such average weekly wage.

There are a variety of other formulas. A number of states use a larger fraction than 1/26, such as 1/25 or even 1/20. Some states use a weighted schedule to give preference to low-income workers

All states have benefit limitations—minimum, maximum, or both Of those states with specified minimums, forty-two have minimums of $10 or less; nine have minimums of $11 to $17 (without dependents). The maximum weekly benefits vary from $26 to $55. The large industrial states generally have higher benefits than the average for all of the states.

Based on the benefit computations previously discussed, and the maximum limitations set forth above, the benefit levels are generally considered to be low. There has been a notable rise in both the maximums provided and the actual average payment in the past twenty years. However, the increases have not kept pace with the increase in wages. Today, with the average weekly wage of covered workers being approximately $90 per week, the average benefit is about 37 per cent of average wages. The Federal administration and many others have been urging states to achieve the goal of 50 per cent of average wages.

By 1960, the maximum weeks of benefits in the various state programs varied from 18 to 39 weeks. Thirty-two states with about 70 per cent of the covered workers in the United States had a maximum duration of 26 weeks; 10 states provided less than 26 weeks; 9 states provided from 28 to 39 weeks.

The continued exhaustion of benefits resulted in Congressional enactment of the Temporary Extended Unemployment Compensation Act of 1961 which became law on March 24, 1961. This temporary extension has resulted in state action to liberalize the number of weeks of duration of benefits.

The burden of unemployment falls most heavily, of course, upon the worker who has other persons dependent upon his income. There has been, therefore, considerable interest in allowing extra benefits for dependents. Today, twelve states have such benefits for dependents.

Financing

The unemployment insurance system is financed completely by the contributions or taxes levied pursuant to Federal law and the various state programs. The contributions are paid almost exclusively by employers. Although the laws of eleven states have in he past provided for employee contributions, only nine ever collected them. Today, only three states collect employee contributions including only two of the original nine states.

When the Social Security Act was first enacted, a difference of opinion arose as to the type of state fund which was to be established. Wisconsin, the pioneer in unemployment insurance legislation, established a separate "reserve account" for each individual employer. It was only from this account that payments could be made to unemployed workers of such employer. In Ohio, a "pooled plan" was developed whereby all contributions were placed in a single state-wide "pooled fund" and all benefits were to be paid out of it. Each system had its defenders and critics among the early leaders and students of social insurance.

The Ohio or pooled plan prevailed. In a social insurance program it became obvious to most of the students of the problem that the risk insured against, namely unemployment, had to be spread among all persons covered. Today all states except two have a pooled fund.

Although Federal law provides for a tax of 2.7 per cent of payroll to be used for payment of benefits, very few employers actually pay such a tax. The average is about 1.7 per cent, and many employers pay substantially less than this average. This situation comes about because of one of the most controversial practices in the unemployment insurance program, namely experience rating. Experience rating is merely a system whereby the tax for an employer is set in accordance with the benefit-payments experience of his employees over a period of time. The theory is that if employers have little or no unemployment, the tax should be reduced in recognition of such fact. Although only three states had experience rating plans in 1940, by 1948 every jurisdiction had some type of experience rating.

States must meet certain minimum Federal requirements before a rate reduction can be granted to an employer. However, the plans vary. Most states (thirty-two) require that the fund must have a certain amount in it before a reduction is made; some states (six) relate it to a ratio to benefits paid; in fifteen states it is related to a percentage of payrolls of past periods; and there are a number of other methods. Twenty-six states permit the employer to increase his reserve and, therefore, lower his contribution rate by making voluntary contributions.

The result of these various plans is that most employers receive substantially reduced rates. These rates vary greatly. During some years individual employers might pay nothing; in some states, provision is made for payment in excess of 2.7 per cent. Minimum rates based on experience ratings range from zero in sixteen states to 1.2 per cent. Maximum rates in the most "favorable schedules" range from 0.5 per cent to 2.6 per cent.

The almost universal use by the states of the experience rating principle is obvious from the previous discussion. Those who favor it maintain that it encourages an employer to reduce separations since lowered unemployment in his business lowers his tax, that rate differentiation is an established and effective insurance principle used in workmen's compensation, that it promotes job security by giving the employer an incentive to keep the worker on the job, and that it prevents fraudulent claims since the employer is interested in preventing fraud which will increase his tax. Those who oppose it maintain that unemployment is generally beyond the power of the individual employer to control, that the financial damage of unemployment is so great that the employer will try to prevent it because of the great general costs thereof as against the minor savings of a reduced unemployment insurance rate, that the analogy to workmen's compensation is unsound since accidents occur in the employer's plant but unemployment is caused by conditions outside of such plant, that employers under experience rating, having an incentive to hold down benefit payments, will discourage the filing of claims, and will try to limit and maintain low benefit provisions. Whatever the merits, as a practical matter, it would appear that experience rating is here to stay.[92] The problem, therefore, is one of developing experience rating so that it will contribute to the basic objectives (rather than detract from them) of unemployment insurance, namely the maintenance of a worker's income at an adequate level during periods of unemployment.

THE FUTURE OF UNEMPLOYMENT
INSURANCE IN THE UNITED STATES

Unemployment insurance has made considerable progress in the twenty-seven years of its existence in the United States. Benefits have been raised and the payment periods have been extended, experience in its administration has pointed up some of the steps necessary to improve the program, and financing methods have emerged which can be the basis of soundly financed future programs. In an average week during 1961, about two-and-a-half million unemployed received benefits, and every community has a public employment office which relates the administration of unemployment benefits to job opportunities. The passage of the Employment Act of 1946 established Federal policy to maintain a high level of employment. Co-ordinated with this policy must be the alleviation of distress due to unemployment. During recent economic recessions, unemployment insurance alone probably offset about one-fifth or even one-fourth of the loss of income. The improvement of unemployment insurance is, therefore, vital not only to the unemployed but to the total economy.

Because of its importance, attention needs to be given to several issues. Coverage should extend to all gainfully employed. Most of the thirteen million employees not covered could be covered without too much difficulty. In respect to the remainder, more intensive study may be needed to iron out what appear to be the obstacles in the way of coverage. An immediate step should be making coverage applicable to employers of one or more throughout the country. Likewise, benefits need to be raised. In 1939, every state except one had maximum benefits which were greater than 50 per cent of the average wage in the state. Today, because of increased wages and the failure to raise benefits accordingly, fewer than ten states have maximums over 50 per cent of average wages. Although there is disagreement as to the exact level at which benefits should be pegged, the fact that a large number of unemployment insurance beneficiaries have been receiving benefits over an extended period of time reinforces the necessity of higher benefits. It was the exhaustion of benefits by many workers that resulted in Congressional action in 1961, to extend the duration of benefits. A minimum benefit, not a liberal one in comparison with that provided by some other systems, would seem to be one which would average at least 50 per cent of the average weekly wage in the state. The impetus of the temporary Federal legislation, already discussed, should lead to a longer period of payment. A benefit duration of at least thirty-nine weeks would appear to be a period which should be adopted by all states.

With reference to financing, the taxable wage base (and therefore benefits) should be raised so that two-thirds to three-fourths of all wages are taxed. An important element of the United States social security system is that its benefits are wage-related. Low maximums tend to blunt this principle and the maximums should be raised and controls over benefit levels established through wage-related formulas. During recent years, several state funds have been weakly financed. This financing needs to be strengthened. Assuming the maintenance of separate state programs and, therefore, separate state funds, some experts have suggested a National Reinsurance Fund to assist recession-hit states during unusual drains on the state funds.[93]

Finally, Federal standards would appear to be necessary. Although the old-age, survivors, and disability insurance program has demonstrated the value of a well-run Federally administered social insurance program, it would appear that unemployment insurance will continue to be a state-administered program. If this is the case, some minimum Federal standards should be established. It is difficult to justify having an employer in one state pay half of the tax of an employer in another state when both employers have the same situation, and the difference in taxes relates to different state formulas. It is difficult, further, to justify a maximum weekly benefit of $36 in the industrial state of Indiana and $50 in the agricultural state of Wyoming; or $35 in Arizona and $55 in the adjoining state of California; or $67 in the New England state of Connecticut and $36 in the New England state of Vermont. Federal standards also should be considered for other aspects of the program which have been presented in the foregoing.

These few comments are merely indicative of some of the next steps; they are not complete. Much progress has, as indicated, been made; much remains to be done to assure every person in America who is unemployed when he is able and willing to work that his income will be maintained on a reasonable level until he is again absorbed in the army of America's seventy million gainfully employed.

"The test of our progress is not whether we add more to the abundance of those who have much; it is whether we provide enough for those who have too little." [94]—*Franklin D. Roosevelt*

CHAPTER VII

PUBLIC ASSISTANCE UNDER THE
SOCIAL SECURITY ACT

The Committee on Economic Security recognized that the original social insurance programs under the Social Security Act were limited and that many persons who were already destitute and in need would not be covered by social insurance for many years to come. Furthermore, it was recognized that social insurance payments would not be high enough in many cases to cover all needs and that public assistance payments would be necessary to supplement social insurance. To round out the program of social security, the Committee recommended Federal financial participation in state programs for needy aged, blind, and dependent children. In mid-1962 over six-and-a-half million needy persons received Federally aided "public assistance" under the Social Security Act.

Public assistance is the term now used to describe state programs for persons who are in financial need and whose financial need is met by the payment of assistance financed in some cases by the Federal Government and the states and localities together or entirely by the states and local governments. Federal financial participation is available under the Social Security Act for five categories:

1. Old-Age assistance. This program provides assistance to needy aged.[95]

2. Medical Assistance for the Aged. This program, effective October 1, 1960, was established by amendments to the Social Security Act enacted in 1960 (Public Law 86–778) to enable states to receive Federal funds for medical care to aged persons not receiving old-age assistance, whose income and resources are not sufficient to meet their medical expenses.

3. Aid to Families with Dependent Children. This program aids certain groups of dependent children.[96]

4. Aid to the Blind. Needy blind are assisted under this program.[97]

5. Aid to the Permanently and Totally Disabled. This program, added to the Social Security Act in 1950, provides assistance to persons who are in need and who have a severe disability expected to be of long duration.[98]

Assistance programs to aid needy persons who are not eligible under the categories of the Social Security Act are supported by state and local funds under programs called "General Assistance," which are discussed in the next chapter.

These public assistance programs under the Social Security Act, providing financial assistance and a variety of services, have been established in all states except four which still do not have Aid to the Permanently and Totally Disabled,[99] and about half of the states which have not yet adopted or implemented the Medical Assistance for the Aged programs. Providing income for over six-and-a-half million aged, blind, disabled, and dependent children, they pay out in assistance over 3.6 billion dollars a year.

These public assistance programs are the subject of considerable discussion and frequent change, and their present status is the result of a long historical development. They are distinguished from the social insurance programs of old-age, survivors, and disability insurance, workmen's compensation, and unemployment insurance by the purposes, coverage, source of financing, and other factors. A primary difference is that social insurance is available to persons who meet the requirements without regard to their need for such benefits; public assistance is available only to those who are destitute or who meet strict standards defining the group of "needy" persons eligible. Public Assistance is paid for from general taxes; social insurance is generally paid for through special taxes or contributions. However, in contradistinction to some "relief" programs, the Federally aided programs provide regular monthly payments to needy persons and such persons have a "right" to such assistance —a right which will be enforced by the courts.

Recognition of governmental responsibility for the destitute preceded programs of social insurance. The relief of destitution has been recognized as a public responsibility since the dawn of civilization. English poor laws were brought over to the American colonies and were the basis upon which modern public assistance programs were built. The poor laws definitely established public responsibility in England and the United States for the care of the poor. Under these laws, responsibility for the care of the destitute was placed upon local communities; to be eligible for aid, a person had to be a resident of the local community; and relatives were held responsible for support of their needy kinsmen. These principles—local administration, legal settlement or residence, and relatives' responsibility—are still dominant principles in the United States public assistance program.

Based on these principles, the American colonies and later the states established a variety of public programs for the care of the poor. Institutions were built for aged and infirm persons and "relief" was given to the poor in their own homes through programs which were frequently called "outdoor relief." In addition, specific "categorical" programs were established to provide special assistance to certain groups such as children of widows and veterans.

The first of these categories were the "mothers' pension acts." A number of sporadic moves had been made in a few states to provide assistance to children in their own homes rather than removing them to institutions for reasons of poverty alone. The movement was given impetus by the White House Conference on the Care of Dependent Children called by President Theodore Roosevelt in January 1909. This Conference urged that children "who are without support of the normal breadwinner should, as a rule, be kept with their parents, such aid being given as may be necessary to maintain suitable homes for the rearing of the children." [100]

This declaration sparked a series of state laws. (For purposes of public assistance and as used in this and the succeeding chapter, the term "state" will refer not only to the fifty states but to four other United States jurisdictions, namely, District of Columbia, Puerto Rico, Virgin Islands, and Guam.) Before the Social Security Act of 1935 all but two states had some type of mothers' aid law.

Special assistance to the aged also made headway, through "old-age pension" proposals. Between 1914 and 1933, 26 states passed old-age pension laws of some kind. In 13 states the "pensionable" age was 70; in 10 it was 65; in 1, 68; and in Alaska, 65 for men and 60 for women.

Provisions for the needy blind also were enacted in many states. By 1933, 23 states had blind pension laws.

These pension laws provided the background for the first three public assistance categories in the Social Security Act: Old-Age Assistance, Aid to the Blind, and Aid to Families with Dependent Children.

Old-Age Assistance

For many years Old-Age Assistance was the largest of the public assistance programs but the lead has now been taken by Aid to Families with Dependent Children. The 2,245,000 Old-Age Assistance recipients (April 1962) are exceeded by the 3,738,000 recipients of Aid to Families with Dependent Children. Since the requirements under the Social Security Act for the operation of the Old-Age Assistance program by the states are similar to those for the other three programs providing cash payments (Blind, Disabled, and Dependent Children), the Social Security Act provisions will be considered in detail at this point.

The Social Security Act did not establish a program of old-age assistance; it merely made it possible for a state to receive Federal funds if the state established one. Providing the state met all of the Federal requirements, the Federal Government would reimburse the state for a portion of its expenditures. Such expenditures are usually given to an eligible recipient in cash, in a regular monthly payment, and in an amount determined by state law and his individual needs and resources. All states now have an Old-Age Assistance program.

All public assistance programs under the Social Security Act must meet certain standard Federal requirements:

1. The person must be in need. The public assistance programs under the Social Security Act are not "pension" programs to persons who reach a certain age or have a specified physical condition, and persons must be without substantial resources as defined by the state.

2. In determining need, the state must consider all income and resources.

3. The state must present a "state plan" to the Federal Government which must set out in detail the laws, regulations, procedures, and practices relating to the state program. The plan must also include a description of the agency's organization and function, the regulations and standards governing personnel administration, reporting and research activities, fiscal operations, and detailed policies governing eligibility for and amount of assistance. This plan must be approved by the Federal Government.

4. The program must be in operation on a state-wide basis. This Federal requirement resulted in extending public assistance to every area and in making it available to persons no matter where they resided in the state. In addition, this requirement effected state-wide standards of assistance as the test of need and as the basis for paying assistance.

5. The state must participate financially, although a state may require localities to contribute to the program. The purpose of this provision was to give the state a financial incentive in the operation of the particular assistance category.

6. The program must be administered by a single state agency or, if administered by local agencies, the state agency must have authority to supervise the local administration of the state's programs and to establish rules, regulations, and standards binding upon the local administration. This "single state agency" concept has resulted in strengthening state public welfare departments. The concept means that a program, e.g., old-age assistance, can be administered or supervised only by one agency. The new program of Medical Assistance to the Aged was placed in Title I of the Social Security Act (the title governing Old-Age Assistance) and, if established, must be administered by the same agency that administers Old-Age Assistance. However, other agencies might handle the other public assistance programs. In practice, practically all states have all the Federally aided assistance programs administered by one state department, or if administered locally, then supervised by one state department.

7. The state must establish methods of administration necessary for the proper and efficient operation of the plan, including the es-

tablishment and maintenance of personnel standards on a merit basis. This requirement was intended to keep politics out of the administration of public assistance, to assure a civil service or merit system in personnel selection, and encourage efficient administration.

8. The State plan must provide for the confidentiality of information obtained about recipients or applicants for assistance. Such information must be used or disclosed only for purposes directly connected with the administration of the program. Since 1951, the names of recipients and the amount of their assistance may be available for public inspection provided that the state's plan includes safeguards against the use of the information for commercial or political purposes.

9. The plan must provide opportunity for all persons to apply for assistance and to have their applications acted upon with reasonable promptness. Federal recommendations encourage all states to act on applications within thirty days.

10. The plan must provide for methods of appeal through a "fair hearing" from the state agency where a claim is either denied or not acted upon within a reasonable time, or the amount of the payment is lower than the claimant contends he is entitled to under the law or if it is suspended or cancelled.

11. The state must submit such reports as the Federal Government may require.

12. Where a needy person receives assistance in an institution, a state authority must be responsible for establishing and maintaining standards governing such institutions. This provision was inserted to protect recipients, particularly the old and infirm, from being housed in substandard institutions. It has contributed to raising the standards of care in both public and private institutions. Persons in public institutions are eligible only if they are patients in medical institutions such as hospitals or nursing homes.

13. The plan must prohibit the receipt of more than one form of Federally aided public assistance. A person receiving Old-Age Assistance, for example, could not also receive blind aid. It does not prohibit, however, different individuals in the same household from receiving public assistance payments under different programs. It is permissible for a recipient of Aid to Families with Dependent Children, Aid to the Blind, or Aid to the Permanently and Totally Disabled

to receive care through the program of Medical Assistance for the Aged.

14. The plan must not impose a residence requirement more restrictive than the maximum in the Social Security Act; namely, residence in the state for five years in the last nine years and for one year immediately preceding application. This applies to Old-Age Assistance, Aid to Blind, Aid to Permanently and Totally Disabled. A one-year residence requirement for the child is the maximum allowed under Aid to Families with Dependent Children; however, if the child is under one year of age, a residence requirement of one year prior to the child's birth may be imposed on the relative.

15. The plan must not have a citizenship requirement barring a citizen who is otherwise eligible; *i.e.*, it could not require that a person be a citizen for a certain specified number of years, or any other such restriction.

16. In Old-Age Assistance, the state plan must not set the eligibility age at more than 65 years.

If a state meets the Federal requirements as set forth above, it has considerable flexibility to establish its own program of Old-Age Assistance and its own standards. The individual states have exercised such prerogative and, as a result, state programs differ with respect to the levels of assistance, residence requirements, citizenship, definitions of need, and other factors.[101] Federal law allows no latitude to the state on matters of age. All states have the required age of 65. There have been occasions when states had special programs for aged under 65, but these programs have not been eligible for Federal participation.

Persons receiving Old-Age Assistance must be in need. The states have wide discretion to determine who is a needy person. The majority of the states have a general standard of need which defines a needy person as one whose income or other resources are insufficient to provide "reasonable subsistence compatible with decency and health." Theoretically, the states develop a budget of need. This budget includes allowances for food, presumed to be based on at least minimum food requirements and priced out in terms of current actual cost; clothing; rent, including utilities; and other items, depending on the state. The other most common items include household supplies, medical care and drugs, and transportation. In actual practice, the standards are frequently developed in relation to the maximum payments permitted by the state law in those states where there is such a legal limitation. Most states develop a complete budget of need for every case even where the maximum payment is too low to permit meeting such need.

After a state has established a standard, need is determined by subtracting income from the amount determined as the need. For example, if in a state the need of the Old-Age Assistance recipient is determined to be $120 a month and the recipient has an income from relatives or a pension or other income of $70, he would receive the difference of $50 from Old-Age Assistance. On the other hand, if the state had a maximum payment of $65, then in that state the person would not be eligible since his income of $70 exceeds the maximum allowed. Some states, however, interpret their maximum as being the maximum amount that the state will pay. In such a state, where the budget of need is $120 and the maximum payment is $65, the person with an income of $70 might still receive $50 because it is less than the maximum state payment of $65 and is the deficit in his budget of $120.

A new principle was introduced into the Federal Old-Age Assistance law by the 1962 amendments, namely, that certain earned income may be disregarded in determining need. Such disregard of certain income had been limited to Aid to the Blind cases heretofore. The 1962 amendments provide that after December 31, 1962, in determining need, of the first $50 per month of earned income, the state agency may disregard not more than $10 thereof plus one-half of the remainder. As an example, suppose X has a budget of needed income of $115 per month and has been earning $60. The state has been paying X $55 (the difference between $115 and $60). Under the new law, the state would disregard the first $10 and one-half of the remainder up to $50. Therefore, one-half of $40, or $20, would be disregarded, or a total of $30. The earnings of $60, therefore, would result in considering only the remaining $30 as income. Subtracting this from $115 (the budget of needed income) would result in a payment of $85 as against $55 under the previous law.

Although income is the major test as to whether a person is needy, all states have specific requirements as to how real and personal property resources will be considered—a requirement of Federal law. If a person has resources in excess of that permitted by his state, he is not in "need" in that state. In all of the states an Old-Age Assistance recipient is permitted to own his own home and still be eligible, but about a third disqualify a person if the value of the home is over a set amount. Real property, other than the home in which the old-age recipient lives, must be "utilized," where practicable, to meet needs, by being either sold, rented, or otherwise made to produce income.

All states permit a person to possess some personal property. Generally, furniture, clothing, and personal effects are not counted. Cash and liquid resources permitted vary by states and range from $100 in New Mexico for a single person to $1,200 in California for each single person. Three hundred dollars to $500 is a common amount for a single person, which is increased for a family unit. Most states permit ownership of an automobile if necessary for essential transportation. Many states provide that assistance may be denied if a person transfers property within a specified period prior to application for assistance with intent to make himself eligible for such assistance.

Under Federal law, states may pay Old-Age Assistance to eligible persons even though they are living in institutions such as homes for the aged. Such institutions must be either private institutions or public medical institutions which maintain medical standards established by a state standard-setting authority.

Most states provide that adult children shall be financially responsible for the support of their aged needy parents; and in some states it is an eligibility factor so that aid may be denied if such children refuse to contribute to support. All the states encourage such support. About a third of the states provide that the state may bring a civil action against nonsupporting children. In some states, the parent may bring a civil action for support against his children; in a few, refusal to support is grounds for criminal action against the adult child.

With the exception of payments for medical care, Old-Age Assistance payments are made in cash. The amount paid is the difference between the "budget of need" or the maximum fixed by law and his other income. Payment is made by check, usually once a month.

Because of the latitude left to the states to develop their own plans, assistance payments vary. In April 1962 the average payment for the country as a whole was $72.24. However, Mississippi had the lowest payment of any state, namely $35.06 (excluding Puerto Rico, Guam, and Virgin Islands); while the highest, Connecticut, had an average of $111.83. This wide variation is caused by a combination of factors: the amounts and items included in the budget of need, the imposition of maximum ceilings, the fact that financial resources of individual states compel a reduction in the payment so that the recipient receives only a fraction of the agreed-upon budget of need, and other factors. In general, it is agreed that average payments are low—much lower than required to maintain a person on a standard of "decency and health."

These averages, of course, are in excess of other income available to recipients. More than 40 per cent of all OAA recipients have cash income, other than assistance, averaging about $39 per month. The major component of such income is OASDI benefits. Nearly a third of all OAA recipients have such benefits and the average monthly amount is $44. In February 1961, 715,000 persons received both Old-Age Assistance and old-age, survivors, and disability insurance benefits. These persons constitute about one out of every fifteen old-age, survivors, and disability insurance beneficiaries aged 65 or over (6.6 per cent) and almost one-third of all persons receiving Old-Age Assistance (31.0 per cent).

Average payments have been increasing every year. In December 1936, the average payment for all cases was $18.79 per month; ten years later, in 1946, it had almost doubled to $35.31; in April 1962, it was $72.24. However, the payments have always been so low that the increase, when related to the cost of living increase and any reasonable standard of adequacy, is still below accepted standards in most of the states, and it is anticipated that this problem will receive increasing attention by Federal and state officials.

Although most states make no effort to recover payments made to Old-Age Assistance recipients from any later income of the recipient, many states will attempt to recover from the recipient's estate.

The advanced age of Old-Age Assistance recipients makes it inevitable that such recipients have significant health problems. Since 1950, there has been Federal sharing in payments which states made to vendors of medical care (doctors, druggists, hospitals, etc.) directly for care given Old-Age Assistance recipients. Such "vendor payments" are an exception to the usual practice of cash payments to the recipient only. Vendor payments were developed because experience indicated that medical expenses frequently could not be provided for satisfactorily in a regular monthly cash payment.

The increased cost of medical care for the aged has resulted in the newest public assistance program under the Social Security Act. In 1960, Title I, under which Old-Age Assistance was established, was amended to include medical assistance to the aged who are not recipients of Old-Age Assistance but who are unable to meet substantial medical bills. This program is known as "Medical Assistance for the Aged."

The program of Medical Assistance for the Aged authorizes Federal grants to the states to assist the states to pay the costs of medical care for persons aged 65 and over who are not recipients of Old-Age Assistance but whose income and resources are determined by the states to be insufficient to meet medical costs. States are free to determine who will be eligible with reference to income. To qualify for Federal matching grants for such Medical Assistance to the Aged, the state must submit a state plan to the Federal Government for approval. Such plan must meet most of the requirements for Old-Age Assistance. However, there are some differences. Medical Assistance for the Aged must include some of both noninstitutional and institutional care and services. The purpose of this provision is to encourage states to emphasize preventive and corrective services and those services which will enable an individual to live in his own home, rather than in an institution. Under Medical Assistance for the Aged, all residents of the state must be eligible. No property lien can be imposed prior to the death of the recipient and no recovery of benefit payments properly made may be had before the death of the recipient and his spouse.

The Medical Assistance for the Aged program was in effect, or about to be launched, in about half of the states in mid-1962. How large the program will ultimately be and how many additional states will establish such a program remains to be seen.

Who is receiving Old-Age Assistance in the United States today? The 2,245,000 recipients (April 1962) are older than the average aged in the country, women far exceed men, they are heavily weighted with persons from rural and small-town areas, their income is very low, and they usually have illnesses or physical disabilities. In contradistinction to beneficiaries of old-age, survivors, and disability insurance, who constitute most of the aged in the United States, the Old-Age Assistance recipients are a much smaller group of needy aged persons. The growth of old-age, survivors, and disability insurance has been a major factor in lowering the percentage of the aged receiving public assistance. In most states and for the nation as a whole the aged population has grown and continues to grow. However, Old-Age Assistance recipients are declining both in numbers and in terms of percentage of the total aged population. In September 1950, there were 2.8 million recipients of Old-Age Assistance and they constituted 22.6 per cent of the aged population over 65; by February 1960, the number had dropped to 2.4 million and the percentage had fallen to 15.1 per cent; by March 1962, the number was 2.2 million and the percentage was 12.9. It would appear that this downward trend will continue. About one in fifteen persons aged 65 to 69 receives Old-Age Assistance compared with three in ten persons aged 80 or more. Half of the recipients are 76 years of age or older, and about one out of seven is 85 years of age or older.

Approximately 66 per cent of the recipients are women. There are three major reasons for the excess of women. One is their greater longevity. On the average, women aged 65 live about three years longer than men aged 65. Since women generally marry a man slightly older than themselves, the average woman must look forward to several years of widowhood. A second reason is that fewer older women are employed than in the case of men. Approximately 40 per cent of aged men have some income from employment whereas only about 12 per cent of older women (over 65) have such income. A third reason also is the lower percentage of women eligible to receive old-age, survivors, and disability insurance benefits because of lack of attachment to the labor market. These factors account for the fact that 43 per cent of the men receiving Old-Age Assistance have cash income other than from Old-Age Assistance but only 30 per cent of the women have such income.

Although 54 per cent of the aged in the United States live in metropolitan areas (an area with a city of fifty thousand or more), the aged on Old-Age Assistance live predominantly in nonmetropolitan counties. About 58 per cent of the Old-Age Assistance recipients reside in nonmetropolitan areas. Almost two-thirds of Old-Age Assistance recipients live in their own homes. If husband and wife are both alive, almost all live in their own household (94 per cent). Where the aged person is not living with a spouse, only about one out of five men and three out of ten women live alone. About one in six lives with a relative; almost 9 per cent live in an institution, mostly nursing homes; and the remainder (about 12 per cent) live in hotels, rooming houses, or with a nonrelative. Approximately one out of five Old-Age Assistance recipients requires considerable care from other people because of some infirmity; one in fourteen is bedridden or chairfast.

Recipients of Old-Age Assistance have very little income outside of their Old-Age Assistance payment except for the 31 per cent of such recipients who also receive old-age, survivors, and disability insurance benefits. The average outside income for the entire Old-Age Assistance caseload in 1960 was $17.82 per recipient per month—cash income of $16.98 and income in kind valued at $0.84. However, old-age, survivors, and disability insurance beneficiaries on the Old-Age Assistance rolls had a cash income averaging $46.26 over and above their Old-Age Assistance payment, of which $44.03 was from old-age, survivors, and disability insurance benefits. The nonbeneficiary recipients had an average cash income of only $5.40.

Financing. The financing of Old-Age Assistance (as well as the other categories) has been complicated and ever-changing.

The Federal Government normally pays 50 per cent of the state and local costs of administration. However, in 1962 an amendment was enacted which provides for a reimbursement of 75 per cent of administrative expenses for those portions of a state's expenditures which meet certain minimum requirements for providing services leading to rehabilitation and self-support. The purpose of this increased Federal reimbursement is to induce the states to emphasize rehabilitation in the administration of public assistance. The 75 per cent provision applies also to Aid to the Blind, Aid to Families with Dependent Children, and Aid to the Permanently and Totally Disabled.

The formula for determining the Federal share of the assistance payment to the recipient has undergone several changes from the very simple arrangement in 1935 which provided for a Federal payment of one-half of the first $30, or a maximum of $15 for a monthly payment. Changes in the formula were made in 1939, 1946, 1948, 1950, 1952, 1956, 1957, 1958, 1960, 1961, and 1962. Prior to the 1961 amendments, the Federal formula which applied to all adult public assistance programs—Old-Age Assistance, Aid to the Blind, and Aid to Permanently and Totally Disabled—provided that the Federal share was 80 per cent of the first $30 per recipient per month by the participating state. The Federal share in the next $35 of the average assistance payment (up to a maximum of $65 exclusive of the special medical care provision in Old-Age Assistance) ranged from 50 to 65 per cent in accordance with relative state per capita income. This complicated formula was designed to assist the low-income states.

Legislation enacted in July 1962 substantially increased the Federal matching share in Old-Age Assistance (as well as the Aid to the Blind and Aid to the Permanently and Totally Disabled) to twenty-nine thirty-fifths of the first $35 of the average monthly payment per recipient; and the maximum for matching is raised to $70 on a permanent basis effective October 1, 1962.

Special Formula for Medical Care for the Aged. Since 1960, special Federal financing arrangements have been available for those states spending money on medical care for the aged on Old-Age Assistance. Prior to 1960, the maximum average monthly payment for Old-Age Assistance in which the Federal Government would participate was $65. This amount included both money payments to the individual and vendor payments for his medical care. Under the 1961 amendments the Federal Government will continue as before, but will pay 80 per cent of the first $31 of the average monthly payment, with variable matching ranging from 50 to 65 per cent in the remaining $35 up to $66 based on the relationship of the state's per capita income to the national per capita income.

If, however, a state has an average payment of more than $66, the Federal Government will participate to the extent that such payment over $66 is for medical care and up to an average of $15 per month per recipient. The Federal sharing in this $15 will differ in different states. It will range from 50 per cent to 80 per cent based on per capita income. The 1962 amendments continued this special financing of medical care for recipients of old-age assistance, except that the $66 maximum is now increased to $70 as previously set forth, and the matching of the $15 per month set forth above would be for a $15 expenditure over and above the $70, so that Federal funds will be available for participation in OAA to a total maximum of $85 per month.

As a result of this Federal sharing in earmarked medical care vendor payments, states have been stimulated to expand their medical care programs. In the calendar year 1961, the Federally aided categories spent $688,297,000 on vendor payments for medical care; $316,479,000 was for medical care for recipients of Old-Age Assistance. More than 60 per cent of the funds spent for medical care for the aged goes for hospitalization and nursing home costs.

In the Medical Assistance for the Aged program previously described, the Federal Government shares in all state expenditures without any limit under a Federal matching percentage which ranges from 50 per cent for the higher than average per capita income states to 80 per cent for the lowest per capita income states.

In terms of dollars, the Federal Government spends approximately $1,188,000,000 annually (1961) on Old-Age Assistance and state and local governments spend approximately $697,000,000, or a total of $1,885,000,000. The Federal share was 42.8 per cent of all Old-Age Assistance payments in 1936; it rose to 48.5 per cent in 1946; to 54.4 per cent in 1956; and was 63.0 per cent in 1961. State and local sharing of the Old-Age Assistance cost has declined. In 1936 the states paid 45 per cent of the costs and local governments paid 12 per cent; by 1946 the state share was 45 per cent and the local share 6.5 per cent; by 1956, the state share was 39.3 per cent and the local share 6.3 per cent. The 1961 proportions were 63.0 per cent Federal, 32.2 per cent state, and 4.8 per cent local. The trend is continuing in the direction of lowering local contributions substantially as between state and local financing and increasing the

Federal share of the total expenditure. Federal funds come from general revenues of the Federal Government and are appropriated annually. The appropriation is of an "open end" type since the Federal Government, by law, is required to match state expenditures; if the number of recipients and state expenditures increase, the Federal funds must be appropriated to meet such increase.

Although both state and local shares have been declining, in dollar terms, the amount is significant. Whereas in 1936 the state-local expenditures were $88.8 million, they rose to $422.3 million in 1946 and $762.4 million in 1956. For 1961, the total was approximately $697,000,000.

Administration. The Federal Government's responsibility in Old-Age Assistance is placed in the Department of Health, Education, and Welfare. The Secretary of Health, Education, and Welfare has delegated most of the authority to carry on all of the public assistance programs to the Commissioner of Welfare, who heads the Welfare Administration, newly established as of January 28, 1963. The Commissioner operates the program through the Bureau of Family Services (formerly the Bureau of Public Assistance). This Bureau maintains a field staff which examines state operations, advises states on technical matters, conducts reviews of various kinds, and carries on other supervisory and consulting functions. It approves state plans and arranges for the transmission of Federal funds to the states; collects and publishes data on the operation of public assistance programs; and provides technical assistance to the states.

In every state, Old-Age Assistance is the responsibility of a state welfare department. These departments are a large and significant part of state government, operating the public assistance programs, a wide variety of child welfare activities, and in some states, institutional programs for delinquents and the mentally ill. The departments are usually called "Department of Public Welfare" or some similar name. In thirty-two states, Old-Age Assistance is a state-administered program entirely; *i.e.*, the state has established its own district offices as local administrative units. In twenty-two states, Old-Age Assistance is a locally administered, state-supervised program. In such states, local cities or counties administer the program with supervision from the state.

There are over three thousand local departments of welfare operated either by local communities or as local offices of a state agency. Frequently there are both, since many states which administer the public assistance programs on a state basis have their general assistance programs (see Chapter VIII) administered by local governments. The local departments are usually called "County Department of Public Welfare" or some similar name.

Aid to the Blind

Aid to the Blind is a public assistance program for needy blind persons. Like Old-Age Assistance, it is a state program, financed in part by Federal funds. In April 1962 these programs were assisting 101,002 blind persons (approximately one-third of the blind in the United States) at a total cost of more than $7,800,000 for that month. Its administration and financing are almost identical to that of Old-Age Assistance. All states have established programs under the Aid to the Blind provisions of the Social Security Act. The general Federal requirements previously discussed under Old-Age Assistance apply also to Aid to the Blind and need not be repeated here. There are, however, a few specific characteristics and requirements.

To be eligible a person must be blind. The definition of blindness is generally what is referred to as economic blindness and does not require complete or total blindness. Many states have established age limits for eligibility. Thirty-one states have no age limit; the rest provide that the blind persons must be over 16, or over 18, or 21; and some require that they be under 65. The reason for age restrictions is the eligibility for other programs; i.e., Old-Age Assistance for the older persons and Aid to Families with Dependent Children for the younger.

Most states use the same tests of need as in Old-Age Assistance. However, under Federal law, the first $85 of monthly earned income must be disregarded in determining need. In addition, one-half of all earned income over $85 must be disregarded. The Public Welfare Amendments of 1962 added another income exemption. A recipient of blind aid participating in a state-approved plan for achieving self-support may have treated as exempt income the amounts which are spent for achieving self-support, if such expenditures are necessary for the fulfillment of the plan for a period not to exceed twelve months.

Maximum payments are similar to Old-Age Assistance; in states where Old-Age Assistance has no maximum, Aid to the Blind usually has no maximum; the maximum is higher in some states than Old-Age Assistance.

Income and property resources permitted generally are the same as Old-Age Assistance, with a few states having more liberal regulations. In April 1962, the average cash payment to 101,000 recipients was $77.41, or about 8 per cent higher than the average of $70.93 for Old-Age Assistance for the same month. There is, however, great state variation. Considering the general need of the blind for extra medical and household expenses, it is generally agreed that this average payment is low and does not meet the minimum standard set by most of the states.

A few states require the blind person to co-operate in a plan for restoration of sight or vocational rehabilitation. The responsibility of relatives is similar to that in Old-Age Assistance, and the financing formula and Federal sharing are the same except for the special medical care provisions for the aged.

It is interesting that there has been a downward movement of the caseload since 1958, reflecting both the growth of old-age, survivors, and disability insurance, the success of the medical profession and industry in preventing blindness, and the increased number of blind who are self-supporting.

Aid to the Permanently and Totally Disabled

Aid to the Permanently and Totally Disabled is the most recently established of the categorical assistance programs. It became part of the Social Security Act pursuant to the Social Security Amendments of 1950.[102] This program was established because of the growing recognition of the needs of disabled people. In 1950 the disability provisions of old-age and survivors insurance had not yet been enacted and the disabled in the country were being taken care of by states and local communities under a generally admitted inadequate general assistance program. There was a great need, therefore, for special assistance to the disabled. This assistance was accelerated by the program of public assistance for the permanently and totally disabled. The development of Aid to the Permanently and Totally Disabled under the Social Security Act has been rapid, and by January 1962 all states except four [103] had a program.

The Social Security Act provides that a person is eligible for Aid to the Permanently and Totally Disabled if he is 18 years of age or older and is "permanently and totally disabled." Most of the states have developed a very strict definition of disability.

As of April 1962, there were 408,604 cases of recipients of Aid to the Permanently and Totally Disabled in the United States. The average assistance payment during that month was $71.89, or about 7 per cent less than the average payment during that month of $77.41 in Aid to the Blind. Total assistance payments for the year 1962 were approximately $350,000,000; approximately 56 per cent was paid from Federal funds and the remainder from state and local funds. Most of the recipients of Aid to the Permanently and Totally Disabled are in late middle life, with about half of them falling in the ages 55 to 64. About 10 per cent are under 35. The most frequently diagnosed impairment is heart disease, but most recipients, because of the very strict definition, which requires great disability and impairment, have more than one disease or impairment. About two out of ten recipients are housebound. The number of persons receiving Aid to the Permanently and Totally Disabled is not expected to increase very much during the next several years because of the impact of disability insurance under the old-age, survivors, and disability insurance program.

Aid to Families with Dependent Children

The program of Aid and Services to Needy Families with Children is the fastest growing public assistance category. Known as Aid to Dependent Children until the 1962 Amendments to the Social Security Act, the name was changed by Congress to reflect the emphasis on the family as a basic unit of concern as well as the emphasis on rehabilitation. Although the official title is "Aid and Services to Needy Families with Children" the text of the new law refers to the program as "Aid to Families with Dependent Children," (AFDC).

Three reasons for dependency will be recognized under the Federal law as it existed prior to 1961:

1. Physical or mental incapacity of a parent
2. Death of a parent
3. Continued absence from the home of a parent

Furthermore, the child must be living in the home of a relative. This is in line with the fundamental goal and purpose of the Aid to Families with Dependent Children law, which is to maintain children in their own homes.

During the past two decades the population of the United States under 18 years of age has increased rapidly. The birth rate has been high, and in the 1960 census there were 64,200,000 children under 18 years of age as compared to 47,000,000 in 1950, and 40,300,000 in 1940. The increase in the child population, as well as a number of other factors, has resulted in the fact that the Aid to Families with Dependent Children program is now the largest, in terms of number of recipients, of any of the public assistance programs in the United States. As of April 1962, there were 3,738,272 recipients representing 955,835 families with 2,889,000 children.

Eligibility for assistance is based on state law subject to certain Federal requirements as in the other categorical assistance programs. About half the states have the maximum age permitted under the Federal law, namely, aid is extended to children up to 18 years of age. Almost half the states provide that aid is extended to children up to 16 years of age, and from then until age 18 if the child is regularly attending school. Need is established in the same manner as in Old-Age Assistance through a budget of needed income. Most states have maximum payments specified by law or regulation. Generally, they provide a maximum per child and a family maximum. In April 1962, the average family payment was $123.92, the average per recipient was $31.68. However, state variations are even greater in AFDC than in the other programs. It is estimated that almost half of all AFDC cases have unmet needs even by the limited standards of some of the states.

Until 1961, a basic element of eligibility was deprivation of parental support or care by reason of death, disability, or continued absence of a parent. In almost all cases, eligibility is based on the status of the father. In 11 per cent of the families, the father is dead; in 65 per cent the father is absent because of divorce, separation, desertion, unmarried parenthood, confinement in an institution, or other reasons; in 22 per cent the father is disabled; and a large variety of reasons account for the remaining 2 per cent. In about nine out of ten AFDC families the mother is in the home; both parents are in the home in about one-fifth of the families. Many states provide that the home must meet standards of "suitability," and a few states have attempted to interpret this so as to exclude cases where the mother does not meet the accepted moral standards of the community. The Congress, however, has held that the purpose of AFDC is to assist all eligible children who are being cared for in their own homes unless a court or other authority has removed the children from their home.

Seventeen states require a parent to accept "suitable" employment; several others have administrative rulings or practices to the same effect. This requirement has given rise to considerable difficulty. Since the purpose of AFDC is to keep mother and child together, particularly when the child is young, the requirement, strictly construed, can militate against the basic purpose of the program. Furthermore, plans must be made for the day care of children if mothers are required to work. In practice, most states do not enforce the requirement in the case of mothers of young children.

Since 1953, the AFDC caseload has risen steadily. The major reasons for the increase are the growth of the child population; growth in the number of families; and higher assistance standards which make more families with some income eligible. Approximately 4.1 per cent of the nation's children are receiving AFDC. Approximately 58 per cent of all AFDC funds come from the Federal Government. Turnover in the caseload is more rapid than in the other Federally aided public assistance categories. The median length of time on AFDC is 2.1 years, and families leave the rolls primarily because the mother remarries, some person in the home finds employment, or the children reach the upper age limit. The median age of the children is 8.8 years. Three-fourths of the children are under 13 years of age. For the nation as a whole, the average AFDC family includes 3.9 persons.

A large number of AFDC families have income other than public assistance to apply against their budgeted needs. A recent study indicated that 45 per cent had some income—averaging $53 per month for these families; 13 per cent of the families had an average of $48 per month from the mother's earnings; 6 per cent had an average of $35 per month from earnings of someone in the family other than the mother; 12 per cent received an average of $51 per month from the father not in the home. Six per cent received an average of $64 per month in old-age, survivors, and disability insurance payments; 10 per cent received an average of $41 per month in cash from other sources; 9 per cent averaged $14 per month from income in kind (grown foodstuffs, housing, etc.).

On May 8, 1961, the President signed into law an enactment which involved a substantial change in the Aid to Dependent Children program previously described.[104] Under the 1961 amendments to the Social Security Act, Title IV is extended so that Aid to Families with Dependent Children payments may be made to assist children who are in need because of the unemployment of a parent. Prior to this amendment, the families of such destitute unemployed persons were cared for through general assistance. The new amendment made Federal assistance available to needy children deprived of parental support or care because of the unemployment of a parent. Previously AFDC was available only to children deprived of support or care because of the death, continued absence, or incapacity of a parent. Federal grants were available for these "unemployment" cases on the same basis as other AFDC cases for the period May 1961 through June 1962. In July 1962, Congress passed a series of amendments to the AFDC provisions of the Social Security Act. One of these amendments extended for a period of five years the temporary provision covering cases where the need of the child is due to unemployment and it expanded the previous provision to cover both parents.

A substantial number of children in foster homes are being assisted by general assistance or other public funds but not by AFDC because they are not in the home of a relative. Many such children received AFDC prior to placement in such homes. In order to allow the states to make more flexible arrangements, the 1961 amendments further amended Title IV for the same temporary fourteen-month period—from May 1961 through June 1962—as for aid to children of the unemployed. The term "dependent child" under these amendments includes a child who would otherwise be a dependent child within the meaning of Title IV except for his removal after April 30, 1961, from his home by a court that has found that it is contrary to the welfare of the child to continue living there; for whose placement and care the AFDC agency is responsible; who as a result of the judicial determination is placed in a foster family home; and who received AFDC in or for the month in which such court action was initiated. This provision was made permanent by the Public Welfare Amendments of 1962. The law requires that the foster family home where the child is placed must be one licensed by the state or approved by the licensing agency of the state as meeting the licensing standards.

The AFDC program has made a substantial contribution in keeping parents and children together; its great weakness has been the lack of services to assist families to overcome the difficulties—economic, social, psychological—which many of them face. The development of more adequate social services is a next step. In the meantime AFDC is helping to bring some measure of economic security to almost a million families and making a substantial contribution to the total United States social security program.

"Few nations do more than the United States to assist their least fortunate citizens—to make certain that no child, no elderly or handicapped citizen, no family in any circumstances in any state, is left without the essential needs for a decent and healthy existence." [105] —*John F. Kennedy*

CHAPTER VIII

GENERAL ASSISTANCE

"General assistance" is the name applied to public programs of assistance to needy persons, financed by state or local funds, and paying benefits either in cash or in kind to persons in need in their own homes or in institutions. It is a "residual" program, covering cases not cared for under the Social Security Act public assistance categories, and in some instances it may supplement the aid received by the individual or family under the Federal public assistance categories. It has been referred to as a "catch-all" program since it may provide for assistance to any needy individual not provided for by other programs. The state and local general assistance programs most resemble the "poor relief" laws inherited from Great Britain. General assistance is financed entirely by state or local funds, there is no Federal participation, standards of assistance are generally lower than in the public assistance categories under the Social Security Act, and eligibility, coverage, standards of administration, financing, and other characteristics vary widely.[106]

The number of cases receiving assistance under the general assistance program varies from year to year and even from month to month. This is due to the fact that employment conditions affect the size of the program more directly than in the categorical programs. Unemployment is a leading cause of receipt of general assistance. The amount of money expended is considerable. In April 1962, a total of $26,457,000 was paid out for general assistance to 379,000 cases, representing 960,000 recipients. The average payment per case was $69.86 for the month.

Originally administered by local communities without state supervision or financial participation, general assistance is gradually moving toward greater state participation. In eighteen states, general assistance is administered entirely by the state through its own offices. In nine states, the state public assistance agency supervises a general assistance agency operated by county or municipal governments. These local agencies usually administer the categories also. In twenty-six states general assistance is administered by local political jurisdictions without state supervision or with very limited supervision. The most common unit of administration is the county, which is the unit used in thirty-nine states. However, ten states have towns or cities as the most common unit; and four states have specially defined areas of the state agency which is the unit of administration.

Eligibility for general assistance varies from state to state and, where administered locally, frequently varies from locality to locality. Generally, the requirement that a person be in financial need is interpreted much more strictly than in the Federally aided assistance programs. Although all states aid needy families, in seventeen states aid may be denied if there is an employable person in the family.

A legacy from the English poor laws has been the concept of residence. Under this concept only persons who have resided in a state or locality for a specified period of time are eligible for general assistance. Sometimes the local or state law requires that during this initial period of establishing residence no public aid must be received. Forty states had a durational residence requirement in 1959. Residence requirements in some states have been liberalized in recent years and it is agreed by most students of general assistance that such requirements should be abolished. They may have had some validity in the early days when migration was negligible and all governmental assistance was given by the local community, with local funds. But twentieth-century America is a nation on wheels. People travel freely and change jobs frequently; persons may live in one state and work in another; national firms may move employees to different states; and a variety of other factors makes residence requirements an outmoded and generally unsatisfactory restriction.

General assistance is a much more limited program than the categorical assistance programs. In twelve states, only emergency or short-term assistance is given; fourteen states restrict aid to special situations such as families with unemployable persons, those with medical care needs, or other special needs, but twenty-seven states will assist all kinds of cases within the eligibility requirements of the particular states. In fourteen states, a maximum is set on the amount of assistance which can be given to a recipient; in most of the remaining states, there is no maximum set but a maximum payment may result if funds are not available. Six states limit the duration of assistance. The remainder have no limitation on duration or else the limitations are set by local communities and are not uniform in the state.

In contradistinction to the Federal public assistance programs where the payment is almost exclusively a cash money payment, in general assistance only about one-half of the states generally use cash money payments. Ten states generally use voucher payments and the remainder use both.

About a third of the states use the same standards of assistance as are used in the public assistance categories. The rest have different, usually lower standards.

General assistance is characterized by a great diversity of eligibility requirements, administrative organization, and the amount of assistance paid to individuals or families. Although the lack of Federal funds does give certain local flexibility (since there is no requirement for state-wide standards or other general regulations), this very factor has prevented general assistance from making even the limited progress of the other public assistance categories. With local tax funds being extremely limited and with the many demands being made upon such local funds for police and fire protection, schools, sanitation, roads, and other major needs, the prospects for substantial improvement in general assistance lie in increased state and Federal funds.

The trend is in the direction of greater Federal assistance. When Aid to the Permanently and Totally Disabled was established under the Social Security Act in 1950, thousands of cases of disabled persons under 65 years of age were transferred from general assistance. In 1961 the addition of the unemployed father case to the Aid to Families with Dependent Children program resulted in more transfers. Whether the Federal Government should expand AFDC to include all needy children (which would cover a large number of general assistance cases) or establish another Federally aided category of general assistance is now the subject of discussion. Whatever changes are made, general assistance probably will remain a small program to care for those not eligible under the Federal categories.

" . . . it is revolting to judgment and sentiment alike that the burden of accidents occurring because of the necessary exigencies of their daily occupation should be thrust upon those sufferers who are least able to bear it." [107] —*Theodore Roosevelt*

CHAPTER IX

Social Insurance Covering Industrial Accident and Disease
(Workmen's Compensation)

Even in the most primitive societies, work was hazardous and many persons were injured, crippled, or killed in the course of such primitive occupations as hunting, tending animals, or planting and harvesting crops. The industrial revolution, however, made work even more dangerous. Mines which might cave in or explode, steel mills where persons might be burned or crushed, skyscrapers and bridges from which workers might fall, high tension electrical wires which upon being touched could electrocute, dust which caused disease—these and hundreds of other hazards began to appear or to be increased in early industrial societies. Indeed, it would appear that modern industrial society assumes the disabling, or crippling, or killing of some of its workers.

Few people realize how large is the number of industrial disabilities and casualties. Even in the United States, with safety programs to protect the worker which are among the best in the world, approximately two million persons are the victims of industrial accidents annually. The death rate in 1960—22 per 100,000 workers —is the lowest since death-rate reporting under the existing reporting plan began in 1936. These work injuries and deaths resulted in about forty-one million man-days of disability in 1960.

Because of the dramatic and easily understood nature of the risks involved in work, insurance to cover work-connected injuries emerged as the first of the large social insurance programs. In earlier industrial societies, accidents were looked upon as part of the risk the worker assumed in consideration of his employment and compensation. Under the English common law and the Napoleonic Code, which governed European countries, an injured workman could sue his employer, but, in order to obtain damages or compensation, the worker had to prove that the employer was at fault. Under the English common law, the employer was required to exercise "reasonable care." If he did this, he could escape liability. Court decisions, both in England and the United States, which adopted the English common law, tended to further excuse the employer on three grounds.[108]

First, the courts held that the worker was free to reject or leave the work, and by accepting employment there was an "assumption of risk."

Second, if a fellow employee was the cause of the accident, the employer was excused. This came to be known as the "fellow-servant rule."

Third, if there was "contributory negligence" on the part of the worker, the employer was not liable. Frequently, it was difficult to prove that the injury did not involve some negligence on the worker's part.

However, the large number of accidents, the increase of litigation, and the hardship and suffering which ensued because of industrial injuries, led to a series of legal enactments and efforts to remedy the situation. These enactments have generally been termed "Workmen's Compensation."

Germany led the way in enacting the first "modern" workmen's compensation. In 1838, workmen's compensation was applied to the Prussian railroads.[109] In 1881, Chancellor Bismarck proposed a comprehensive system of social insurance which embodied in it an "Accident Insurance Act" passed in 1884. Similar in concept and administration to other parts of the Chancellor's social insurance "package," it was compulsory, contributory (requiring contributions of both employer and employee), and provided for a great deal of centralized government control. The German experience was so successful that by 1910 almost all European countries had adopted similar legislation.[110]

In the meantime an entirely different approach was being developed in England. Starting in 1846 when Parliament enacted a law giving survivors of deceased employees the right to claim compensation, efforts were made to abolish the defenses of assumption of risk. The British system differed from the German in many respects. Whereas the German program was compulsory, the British was elective; whereas the German system provided for centralized government administration, the British left the administration to the courts; whereas the financing of the German system was through government supervised nonprofit insurance funds, the British system provided for insurance through private insurance companies.

In contradistinction to old-age, survivors, and disability insurance, which borrowed heavily from the German concepts, workmen's compensation in the United States was influenced more by the British system. Workmen's compensation is a state program (except for Federal laws relating to Federal Government employees); there is no Federal supervision; state laws have many elective features; and a great portion of the insurance is carried by private insurance firms.

Both the German and British experiences were watched with interest in the United States by government officials. While the labor unions, prior to 1900, were concentrating on the strengthening of employer's liability acts, officials of the United States Bureau of Labor and of state labor bureaus were studying the European programs.

The modern workmen's compensation movement in the United States may be said to have started in 1908.[111] Before then, civil employees of the Federal Government were not even protected by the older state employer liability acts. President Theodore Roosevelt had long advocated workmen's compensation laws. Congress enacted on May 30, 1908, the first law, which withstood later court attack, covering Federal civilian employees. This law sparked nation-wide interest and action. In 1910 and 1911, eleven states passed compensation laws; four more followed in 1912; seven more in 1913; two in 1914; seven states, Hawaii, and Alaska in 1915; and five more in 1917. In all, thirty-eight jurisdictions established state laws in seven years. Today, every state has a workmen's compensation law.

Workmen's compensation is based on the principle of "liability without fault." Its major objective is the payment of benefits to workers or survivors of workers for work-connected injuries or death irrespective of fault on the part of either the employer or employee. It is a method of maintaining income where such income is lost due to work-connected disability, and is similar to other income maintenance programs such as old-age or survivors insurance under the Social Security Act. It is a form of social insurance.[112] However, it goes beyond the other social insurance programs and includes a theory of "damages," i.e., the employer should pay damages for injuries sustained on the job. The courts have applied a number of theories to justify workmen's compensation laws. Most prominent is the doctrine of "trade risk" or "occupational risk" which holds that the economic loss of work-connected injury is a proper charge on the cost of doing business. It is based on the "status" of the worker. Just as in old-age insurance under the Social Security Act where eligibility to old-age benefits depends upon "insured status," in workmen's compensation it is the status as an employee which produces the entitlement to compensation.

Under these legal theories, the early proponents of workmen's compensation hoped and expected that every work-connected injury would receive adequate and appropriate compensation. However, this has not always been the case.[113] Differing state laws, court decisions, and varying administrative practices have sometimes limited workmen's compensation awards to less than the worker might have received under the old employer's liability laws.[114] Lord Beveridge, in his famous report,[115] urges that workmen's compensation be included "within the general framework of social insurance." At present, it would appear that workmen's compensation will remain a state program, rather than within the framework of the Federal social security program.

Although all states have workmen's compensation laws, coverage is not as extensive as under old-age, survivors, and disability insurance. No state law covers all employment. The characteristics of state laws may be summarized under six headings:

1. Compulsory or Elective. As of January 1, 1960, twenty-five states had compulsory laws and twenty-five had elective laws.[116]

2. Number Covered. It is difficult to obtain an accurate estimate of the number covered by state laws. However, it would appear

that approximately 80 per cent of all employees in the United States come under the protection of workmen's compensation laws.

3. Exclusions. Employers in twenty-eight states need not insure their employees if they employ fewer than the required number, usually less than three.[117] In only eleven states is coverage compulsory for all employees [118] of employers in specified covered occupations. There is also wide variation in occupations not covered. Most states exclude "casual employees"; the majority also exclude domestic and agricultural workers; some exclude nonprofit organizations. The trend is definitely toward extension of coverage to occupations heretofore excluded. Most of the laws provide coverage for governmental employees. Minors, originally excluded from some statutes, are now covered by all states. Railroad workers are not covered under state workmen's compensation laws, but rather are protected by a special Federal law of the employer's liability type. Originally, many states excluded occupational diseases as contrasted to occupational accidents; today, however, all but two states include disease in their coverage. In most states where a specific occupational disease is not included, the employer may be liable under common law or employer's liability laws for damages.

4. Benefits. In any one week, approximately 500,000 persons receive workmen's compensation benefits.[119] Originally limited to cash benefits, the programs now include payment for medical care and rehabilitation. Cash payments, sometimes referred to as "indemnity payments," are designed to replace income lost by reason of disability or death and/or to compensate the worker for the disability, or surviving dependents in case of death. In general, payments are made for death and for four types of injuries: permanent total disability, permanent partial disability, temporary total disability, and temporary partial disability.

The amount of cash indemnity benefits to workers is set in most states as a percentage of average wages, but with dollar maximums, which in many states are set so low as to provide significantly lower benefits as a percentage of wage for workers with wages at the average level or higher. The percentage for temporary total disability (the most common category) is 60 to 66-2/3 per cent for workers without dependents in almost all states; in five states (with less than 3 per cent of the covered workers), it is less than 60 per cent, and in two states, it is in excess of 66-2/3 per cent. In six states, a higher percentage is paid for temporary total disability if the worker has dependents, while in a few states flat supplements are paid for dependents. All states which compute benefits as a percentage of wages have a maximum weekly payment—about one-quarter of the states have a maximum weekly benefit for temporary total disability (including any dependents allowances) of less than $35, while at the other extreme, fifteen states have a maximum of $55 or more. Some states have a higher maximum on the weekly benefit for temporary total disability for workers with dependents than for those without dependents (even though the percentage benefit rate may be the same for all workers). A minimum weekly payment is also established in most of these jurisdictions. Benefits vary according to the classification of injury. In general, it may be said that benefits for temporary total disability for the country as a whole approximate 50 per cent of average wages for workers without dependents (and a little higher when dependents allowances are considered).

Benefits for temporary total disability are payable only after a waiting period (except in Oregon); this is seven days in thirty-four states and two to four days in other states. Benefits are payable for a specified period of time or in a maximum dollar amount. Approximately one-half of the states provide benefits for life; others range from 300 weeks to 1,000 weeks. The total dollar payments are limited from a low of $10,000 in several states to over $45,000 in Michigan.

Death benefits to survivors likewise are generally based on a percentage of wages, and maximum dollar amounts are applicable as well as a maximum period. Generally lower than payments to the worker for disability, the benefit rates, before the application of dollar maximums, average about 50 per cent of earnings for widows and 66-2/3 per cent for a widow with children. Most of the states have maximum benefit periods usually running from about seven to ten years and maximum amounts generally from $10,000 to $12,000.

Although some laws carried provisions for medical care from the very beginning, it was not until 1930 that all states provided for some form of medical treatment. Medical care payments are now an important and significant part of the workmen's compensation program and account for about one-third of total benefits. Increasing, also, is the role of rehabilitation programs. Almost half of the states provide payments during rehabilitation or retraining.

5. Financing. The benefits are paid for by the employer,[120] who may insure either with a private insurance company or a state fund, or be self-insured, except in eight states where employers are required to insure with the state fund.

6. Administration. Workmen's compensation is generally administered by special state boards or commissions. In some jurisdictions the board or commission is in the department of labor, in others they are independent, and in a few states the courts administer the program.[121]

With all its defects and limitations—lack of complete coverage, low benefits, and other aspects—workmen's compensation does protect the large majority of workers from the stoppage of income during periods of work-connected disability and provides medical benefits for those needing them. However, workmen's compensation, the earliest of the social insurance programs in the United States, has developed along lines quite different from other social insurance measures under the Social Security Act.

Many problems still remain to be solved. Although the United States programs of safety and accident prevention have increased and generally are as good as those of any other country in the world, much yet remains to be done to expand and improve in this area; the numerous exclusions need to be eliminated both as to covered employments and covered disabilities; benefits need to be increased to keep up with the increased cost of living; and many of the maximums (both on benefit amounts and on benefit durations) should be increased or abolished completely.

"The true history of the United States is the history of transportation." [122] —*Philip Guedalla*

CHAPTER X

ECONOMIC SECURITY PROGRAMS
FOR RAILROAD WORKERS

Railroad workers occupy a special and perhaps privileged role in the social security program of the United States. The old-age, death, and disability benefits for railroad workers are co-ordinated with the social security program of old-age, survivors, and disability insurance but at the same time have aspects of private or industrial pension and insurance plans. As a result of the historical development of the Railroad Retirement program, railroad workers have greater protection under social insurance than any other large group of workers in the United States.[123]

The first formal private pension plan in the United States was established in 1875 by the American Railway Express Company for railroad workers. By 1934, the railroad industry was in the forefront of industrial pension plans. However, the plans were not fully funded and their financing generally could not withstand the onslaught of the Great Depression. Congress felt that the economic situation necessitated some measure to save these retirement systems and in 1934 established the first important Federal legislative enactment of old-age security in the United States by passing the Railroad Retirement Act.[124] The Act established contributory old-age pensions for employees of railroads, sleeping-car companies, and express companies. In 1935, the United States Supreme Court declared the Act unconstitutional in a famous five-to-four decision, on the grounds that "the act is not in purpose or effect a regulation of interstate commerce" and that several provisions took property without due process of law.[125] A second Railroad Retirement Act was passed by Congress in 1935 similar to the first; it was declared unconstitutional as to its tax provisions by the Supreme Court of the District of Columbia, but because of certain unsettled aspects the system started operating on a small scale. President Roosevelt called the railroad companies and the railroad labor organizations together to obtain an area of agreement for establishment of a mutually acceptable plan that would not be declared unconstitutional. In 1937, Congress enacted another, slightly different, retirement system embodying such agreement, and this forms the basis of the present law, although it has been amended many times during the past twenty-five years.

In general, the employees of all railroads engaged in interstate commerce (including the Railway Express Company and The Pullman Company), and employees of railroad associations and railway labor organizations are covered by the railroad social insurance plan. Five types of benefits are provided: retirement, survivor, disability, unemployment, and sickness and maternity. The first three types of benefits listed are provided by the Railroad Retirement Act, and the latter two types are provided under the Railroad Unemployment Insurance Act.

Retirement Benefits. Old-age annuities are payable upon retirement at age 65 if the railroad worker has at least ten years of service in covered railroad or related work. At ages 60–64, a worker may receive such annuity after thirty or more years of service, but the annuities are reduced for men. Women get the full annuity even if they retire at ages 60–64 if they have thirty or more years of service. Both men and women may retire at ages 62–64 with ten years of service with a reduced annuity.

The amount of the retirement benefit is related to average pay over the entire period of railroad service and to years of service. It is important to note that, unlike what is done under old-age, survivors, and disability insurance, railroad service before 1937 is creditable for those who were in an employment relation with a railroad on the enactment date of the 1935 legislation. This is possible for railroad employment because records of such service had been maintained by the railroads. The benefit formula is weighted so that, based on the same period of creditable service, those with lower earnings receive relatively larger benefits than those with high earnings. The law also contains a provision which guarantees railroad employees and their families that their total benefits will be not less than 110 per cent of the amount (or of the additional amount) they would receive if the employee's railroad service had been covered by the OASDI provisions of the Social Security Act. If an employee has less than ten years of railroad service when he retires, he is not entitled to benefits under the Railroad Retirement Act, but his credits are transferred to the OASDI system.

Benefits are based on average earnings for the months of railroad service worked up to certain maximums. Earnings prior to July 1954 may be counted up to $300 per month, earnings between July 1954 through May 1959 up to $350 per month, and earnings after May 1959 up to $400 per month.

Having arrived at the average monthly earnings, the retirement benefit is established by applying the following formula to the monthly compensation: 3.35 per cent of the first $50; 2.51 per cent of the next $100; and 1.6 per cent of the remainder, the sum of these three amounts being multiplied by the years of service. No more than thirty years are creditable if any service before 1937 is used; thus, until 1937, no worker can have more than thirty years of credited service. This formula, unlike that under old-age, survivors, and disability insurance, relates benefit amounts directly to length of covered service, just as is done in most private pension or staff retirement plans.

The maximum benefit payable as of January 1962 was $216.80. This maximum will slowly increase until 1967, and then will increase more rapidly (as more than thirty years of service can be credited). The eventual "practical" maximum (based on fifty years of service at an average wage of $400, payable in the year 2009) is $418, or more than the maximum creditable monthly wage.

A railroad employee with ten years of service may qualify for an unreduced annuity at age 65, or a reduced annuity at age 62. A female employee with thirty years of service may receive an unreduced annuity at age 60. A male employee with thirty years of service may receive a reduced annuity at age 60.

Benefits are reduced 1/180 for each month that an employee who elects a reduced benefit is under age 65 when the annuity begins—

the same reduction percentage as for a worker under the old-age, survivors, and disability insurance system.

An employee's wife or husband is entitled to monthly benefits under specified conditions. The amount of the benefit payable to a spouse is equal to one-half of the employee's annuity, prior to any reduction for the employee retiring before age 65, and then subject to a maximum benefit provision (not more than 110 per cent of the maximum possible old-age, survivors, and disability insurance wife's benefit payable) and to any reduction for the spouse being under age 65 at time of claim.

The retirement benefits and disability and survivor benefits were paid to 906,000 persons during the fiscal year ended June 30, 1961. Such benefits amounted to $987 million. Of this amount retired and disabled employees and their wives received 77 per cent and survivors received 23 per cent. About 397,000 workers were receiving retirement and disability annuities averaging about $133 per month. Disability benefits were lower than age-retirement benefits primarily because, on the average, they were based on a shorter period of creditable service. About 165,000 wives (and husbands, in a few cases) of annuitants were receiving benefits averaging about $58 per month.

Survivor Benefits. Survivors benefits are similar to those of the old-age, survivors, and disability insurance program. Service under both programs is combined in determining both eligibility for survivors benefits and the amount of the benefits. Benefits are payable to:

1. The widow at age 60, or regardless of age if she is caring for a child of the worker;

2. The widower at age 60 if he was dependent upon the wife for at least one-half of his support when she died or retired;

3. Each dependent child if the child is unmarried and is either under age 18 or became totally and permanently disabled before age 18;

4. Each dependent parent at age 60 if the parent was dependent upon the worker for at least half of his or her support at the time of the worker's death.

In addition to monthly annuities, survivors are entitled to two types of lump-sum benefits:

1. An "insurance lump-sum" is payable to the surviving spouse or to the person paying the funeral expenses if no member of the family is entitled to a survivor annuity at the time of the worker's death. For this lump-sum benefit, the worker must have had at least ten years of railroad service and a current connection with the railroad industry.

2. A "residual payment" is payable to any person designated by the worker.

As of June 1961, monthly survivor annuities were being paid as follows:

Figure 4

Railroad Retirement Monthly Survivor Beneficiaries and Average Payment, June 1961

Category	Number of Beneficiaries	Average Monthly Payment
Aged Widows and Widowers	208,400	$65
Widowed Mothers	11,500	86
Children	40,200	57
Parents	1,000	67

Disability Benefits. Disability benefits in the same amount as full retirement benefits (prior to reduction for early retirement) are payable to disabled workers. There are two kinds of annuities payable on account of disability. An "occupational disability annuity" is payable to a worker who is permanently disabled for work in his regular railroad occupation, had a current connection with the railroad industry at retirement, and had twenty years of railroad service (or, if he is 60 years of age or over, had ten years of railroad service). A "total disability annuity" is payable at any age after ten years of railroad service if the worker is permanently disabled for all regular work.

Unemployment Benefits. Railroad workers have a special system of unemployment and sickness insurance. A worker is eligible to draw cash benefits if he is unemployed providing he is able to work, is ready and willing to work, is looking for work or expecting to return to work soon, and is registered with an unemployment claims agent.

All workers covered under the Railroad Retirement system are also covered under the Railroad Unemployment Insurance Act. To be eligible for benefits, a worker must have earned at least $500 in the calendar year before the preceding July 1.

Benefit Amount. The amount the worker receives is based upon his "base year wages." Under present law, the base year wages are counted only up to a maximum of $400 per month. The benefit is based on a daily benefit table. (Figure 5 below.)

Figure 5

Daily Benefit Rate—Railroad Unemployment Insurance

If wages in base year were:			The daily benefit rate for unemployment benefits (also sickness benefits) is:
$ 500	to	$ 699.99	$ 4.50
700	to	999.99	5.00
1,000	to	1,299.99	5.50
1,300	to	1,599.99	6.00
1,600	to	1,899.99	6.50
1,900	to	2,199.99	7.00
2,200	to	2,499.99	7.50
2,500	to	2,799.99	8.00
2,800	to	3,099.99	8.50
3,100	to	3,499.99	9.00
3,500	to	3,999.99	9.50
4,000 and	over		10.20

However, if the amount resulting from the above benefit table is less than 60 per cent of the employee's daily rate of pay for his last railroad employment in the base year, such 60 per cent is used as the daily benefit rate (but subject to a maximum of $10.20).

In each fourteen-day claim-period, the worker is paid for all days of unemployment over four, including Saturdays and Sundays. Benefits can extend for as many as 130 days in the benefit year. If normal benefits are exhausted, a worker with ten years or more of service may get benefits for an additional period. The extended benefit may be paid for an additional 65 days if the worker has ten to fourteen years of service or 130 days if the worker has fifteen or more years of service.

Benefits are reduced if the worker also receives old-age, survivors, and disability insurance benefits, a pension or annuity or other retirement pay under a Federal, state, or local law such as a Railroad

Retirement annuity, a policeman's or fireman's pension or similar pension, certain workmen's compensation payments, or any other social insurance payment under any law.

In calendar year 1960, about 1.13 million railroad employees earned at least the minimum of $500 necessary to qualify for sickness and unemployment benefits in fiscal year 1961. In this fiscal year, about 319,000 persons (or 28 per cent of the eligibles) drew unemployment benefit payments totalling $207 million. The average weekly payment was $40.

Sickness Benefits. Sickness benefits are paid to workers who are temporarily sick or injured and therefore unable to work. The program was established by the Railroad Unemployment Insurance Act, and most of the provisions relating to unemployment insurance apply also to sickness benefits. Benefit amounts are the same. The worker cannot draw sickness benefits if he receives wages, salary, pay for time lost, vacation pay, or other remuneration. However, payments under a private health or accident policy or employer's group insurance policy will not prevent payment of sickness benefits.

In fiscal year 1961, about 128,000 railroad workers (or 11 per cent of the eligibles) received sickness benefits, totalling $55 million. The average weekly payment was $46, and 87 per cent of all beneficiaries received payments at the maximum rate of $10.20 per day.

Maternity benefits for women workers (not for wives of railroad workers) are payable in addition to sickness benefits. Such maternity benefits are payable for a maximum of 116 days in a benefit year, but the benefit rate for the first fourteen days of a maternity period and for the first fourteen days after the birth are at a 50 per cent higher rate, so that in effect 130 full days of benefits are payable. Approximately 3,200 women workers received such benefits in fiscal year 1961 (about 5 per cent of all eligibles), totalling about $3.4 million. The average weekly payment was about $70.

A special system is established for work-connected injury or other disability of railroad workers, but these are offset against the payments available under the temporary disability or sickness program under the Railroad Unemployment Insurance Act. Unlike other workers plans, the typical workmen's compensation program does not apply. Long before effective workmen's compensation programs were established by most of the states, the railway workers secured the enactment of the Federal Employers' Liability Act of 1908. Under this Act, railroad workers must sue the railroads in court; they cannot receive awards through administrative procedures similar to workmen's compensation. Furthermore, there is no "liability without fault" as in workmen's compensation. The worker has the responsibility for establishing negligence, but the common law defenses by the employer of negligence by a fellow servant and assumption of risk have been abolished. Contributory negligence of the worker, likewise, will not defeat a claim; it will merely reduce the award made. Most compensation under this law is awarded pursuant to jury determinations. Although it would appear that this method of compensating for work-connected disability has not caught up with modern trends in workmen's compensation, railroad workers feel that the failure of workmen's compensation to keep abreast of changes in the cost of living makes the present railroad system superior in terms of adequacy of compensation or benefits.

FINANCING RAILROAD RETIREMENT AND UNEMPLOYMENT INSURANCE BENEFITS

The system of retirement, disability, and survivor benefits is financed by taxes set up in the Railroad Retirement Tax Act. The total tax rate, prior to June 1959, was 12-1/2 per cent of the worker's earnings in railroad employment, but not including earnings over $400 per month.[126] Beginning June 1959, the tax rate was 6-3/4 per cent for workers and employers or a total of 13-1/2 per cent combined through 1961. The tax is 14-1/2 per cent for 1962–64. After 1964, the tax will be increased by an amount "equal to the number of percentage points by which the then current social security rates on employers and employees combined exceed 5-1/2 per cent." This means a combined employer-employee rate of 16-1/4 per cent in 1965, 17-1/4 per cent in 1966–67, and 18-1/4 per cent in 1968 and after.

In spite of the projected tax increase, the Railroad Retirement system has not been in actuarial balance; even the new tax rates set forth above will leave an actuarial deficiency, according to the

Eighth Actuarial Valuation of the Railroad Retirement System, of almost 1-3/4 per cent of payroll.

The Internal Revenue Service of the United States Treasury collects the taxes under the Railroad Retirement Tax Act, transfers the funds to a railroad retirement account in the United States Treasury, and invests the funds in special issues (at an interest rate of 3 per cent) or in other United States obligations which are guaranteed as to both principal and interest by the United States and earn at least 3 per cent interest. Interest earned on these securities makes up a significant portion of the total income of the system.

In the fiscal year 1961 (July 1960 through June 1961), the Railroad Retirement Account had income of $1,023 million and outgo of $996 million so that its size changed but little over the year (being about $4.0 billion at June 30, 1961). Almost all of the outgo was for benefit payments. The income consisted of $570 million in contributions, $116 million in interest on investments, and $337 million in transfers from the old-age, survivors, and disability insurance system under the financial interchange provisions.

Each year Congress appropriates funds out of the Railroad Retirement Account for the administration of the railroad retirement program. Administrative expenses under the Railroad Retirement Act during fiscal year 1961 amounted to $9.6 million or 1 per cent of total expenditures.

The Railroad Retirement Board and the Secretary of Health, Education, and Welfare are required to make annual determinations of the amounts which would place the old-age, survivors, and disability insurance trust funds in the same position they would have been in if railroad employment had always been covered by the Social Security Act. In effect, these cost provisions constitute a method of partially reinsuring railroad benefits under the OASDI program. In other words, OASDI in effect receives from the railroad retirement account contributions with respect to railroad service and pays benefits based on railroad service. In some cases these benefits are paid directly to beneficiaries by OASDI, while in other cases they are credited to the Railroad Retirement Account.

The unemployment and sickness benefit programs are financed entirely by railroad employers through contributions paid directly to the Railroad Retirement Board. Employer contributions for both programs combined are set forth in the Railroad Unemployment Insurance Act. Under "permanent" law, contributions are now a maximum of 3.75 per cent of payroll up to $400 per month for each worker. An additional one-quarter per cent was payable in 1962–63 to finance the additional cost of extended benefits similar to those provided in the state systems. The taxes have increased over the years. (Figure 6 below.)

Figure 6

Railroad Unemployment Insurance Tax Rate

Calendar Year	Tax Rate
1957	2.0 per cent
1958	2.5
1959 (first 5 months)	3.0
June 1959 and after	3.75

The exact amount paid by employers for any calendar year depends on the balance in the Railroad Retirement Unemployment Insurance account on the preceding September 30, according to a schedule in the law. All contributions or taxes are paid into the Railroad Unemployment Insurance Account (the benefit account). In addition, interest on funds deposited in the United States Treasury is added, as well as any excess in funds set aside for administration. Such administrative funds are set up in the Railroad Unemployment Insurance Administration Fund. Administrative costs for the fiscal year 1961 amounted to $9.7 million for unemployment insurance and sickness insurance operations. This amounted to 3.6 per cent of the benefit payments for the year. In fiscal year 1961, contributions for unemployment and sickness benefits amounted to $161 million, while benefit outgo was $262 million. The deficit of $100 million was made up by borrowing (according to law) from the Railroad Retirement Account, since the Railroad Unemployment Insurance Account was "in the red" at the start of the year, and on June 30, 1961, the total debt amounted to $201 million.

"Government is a trust, and the officers of the government are trustees; and both the trust and the trustees are created for the benefit of the people." [127]—*Henry Clay*

CHAPTER XI

GOVERNMENT EMPLOYEE
RETIREMENT SYSTEMS

Almost all of the permanent employees of the Federal, state, and local governments are covered by special retirement systems. The retirement systems resemble the industrial pension plans in private industry. In addition, many government employees are covered by old-age, survivors, and disability insurance. Of the total of 11,510,000 employees in the civilian and armed services of government, over 90 per cent are under retirement programs. (See Table IV, Appendix.)

Retirement programs for government employees preceded the Social Security Act; yet, although a few scattered plans for specific employees can be traced back for more than one hundred years, comprehensive public retirement plans in the modern sense are relatively new. The oldest plan in the United States is probably the teachers' pension plan of New Jersey, which began in 1896. General state employee retirement plans began in Massachusetts in 1911; policemen and firemen retirement plans may be said to have begun in Philadelphia in 1916, although a number of older plans provided some partial coverage. The largest of such public plans, that covering Federal Government workers, was established in 1920. In the same year both New York State and New York City established retirement systems for their employees.

From these beginnings the public retirement programs grew rapidly. Whereas, in 1935, only 2.3 million persons were covered by public-employee retirement plans, this had increased to 6.9 million by 1955.[128] During 1961, over 1,500,000 persons were receiving retirement, disability, or survivor benefits from a public employees retirement system. (See Table V, Appendix.) Of this number, approximately 233,000 survivors of deceased government employees drew survivor benefits. The Federal Government programs account for 55 per cent of the total number of beneficiaries out of some 2,300 separate public employee retirement programs. The remaining 45 per cent were beneficiaries under state and local government plans. In 1961, the Federal civil service retirement system alone paid 30 per cent of all public employee benefits to 36 per cent of all beneficiaries. (See Table VI, Appendix.)

The growth of these public programs is evident when notice is taken of the fact that the total benefits increased in just three years from $2,153 million paid out in 1958 to $3,014 million in 1961.

It is difficult to characterize the various public employee retirement programs. All provide for retirement benefits, but the provisions as to retirement age vary greatly. For dangerous occupations such as those of policemen and firemen, the employee under some plans may retire at any age after twenty years of service. Generally, retirement is provided for at a minimum age ranging from 60 to 65, with provision for a reduction in benefits for retirement before that age. Most of the plans have disability benefits, and some have monthly survivor benefits.

The majority of the plans are contributory. Such plans almost always guarantee the participant that benefits will be at least as large as employee contributions paid. A typical contributory plan might be said to be one where the employee pays about 6 per cent and the government agency about 8 to 12 per cent of payroll. Most plans provide for retirement benefits of about 50 per cent of the highest five-year average wage after thirty years of service, although the Federal Government program is substantially more liberal, and a large number of local plans are much less liberal. Local plans generally provide much lower benefits than state or Federal plans. Although the majority of plans are contributory, the large retirement program of the Armed Forces, which is noncontributory but is supplementary to the old-age, survivors, and disability insurance system, makes the total number of beneficiaries of public-employee noncontributory systems loom large.

At the beginning of 1961, 60 per cent of state, county, and local government employees were covered by old-age, survivors, and disability insurance. (See Table VII, Appendix.)

The Federal Employees Civil Service Retirement System

Although some state employee retirement programs might be considered superior to that of the program for Federal Government employees, it may be of interest to summarize the Federal program, since its provisions strongly influence the direction and trend of other public retirement programs and, in general, it is an excellent public retirement system.

The Federal Civil Service Retirement System is a contributory system. The employees pay 6-1/2 per cent on all wages. There is no wage ceiling as in old-age, survivors, and disability insurance. The government departments match this contribution. The additional funds necessary to pay benefits are made available by Congressional appropriation. It is estimated that the government should pay annually about 8 per cent of payroll into the system to cover costs not met by the contributions of employees and government agencies. Today, the system covers almost two million employees. The funds collected are deposited in the Civil Service Retirement and Disability Fund and are invested in government securities. The program is administered by the United States Civil Service Commission.

Several different types of benefits are provided. The most extensive benefit is that of old-age or retirement annuities. Although Federal employees have a compulsory retirement provision at age 70, most Federal employees (about 80 per cent) retire under various optional provisions. With thirty or more years of service, an employee may retire at age 60 (or at age 55, with a reduction of 5 per cent); with five to twenty-nine years of service, at age 62. The maximum retirement benefit must not exceed 80 per cent of the highest five consecutive years of earnings.

Employees who have worked for five years or more and become disabled receive as a disability pension the same amount as the retirement benefit with a minimum benefit guaranteed. The minimum benefit is 40 per cent of the highest five-year average yearly pay, but not more than he would get on the basis of this salary and the total service he would have if he worked until age 60.

Widows receive benefits determined from the employee's benefit, while child survivors generally receive flat amounts irrespective of the deceased worker's salary or length of service. The employee must have been employed for at least five years and at his death must be an employee or in receipt of retirement or disability benefits.

Federal employees not covered under civil service retirement or another Federal staff retirement system are covered by old-age, survivors, and disability insurance. The more than two million Federal government employees who are under the civil service retirement system constitute the largest group of workers not under old-age, survivors, and disability insurance. For many years, organizations representing Federal employees opposed the extension of social security coverage to Federal employment. Opposition of these employee groups apparently has stemmed from fear that social security coverage would tend to delay desired improvements in the civil service retirement system. In recent years a number of the large employee groups have gone on record as favoring social security coverage for Federal employees, but remain opposed to any adjustment in the retirement system to take account of the fact that Federal employees would also have protection under social security. The organizations of Federal employees are apparently not impressed with the successful integration of many local and state employee systems, as well as plans of private employers, with old-age, survivors, and disability insurance. Some have advanced the argument that the Federal retirement system is already adequate and need not be integrated with old-age, survivors, and disability insurance. This ignores the fact that a large number of Federal employees leave government service to go into private industry. Their Federal service has not counted toward old-age, survivors, and disability insurance, and they are thus at a disadvantage. Coverage of this large group of Federal employees under old-age, survivors, and disability insurance continues to be the subject for discussion and study.

"What can a sick man say, but that he is sick?" [129] —*Samuel Johnson*

CHAPTER XII

DISABILITY AND SICKNESS BENEFITS

Programs to protect individuals against the loss of income and costs of medical care due to disability and sickness are among the oldest of the social insurance and voluntary insurance programs. Such insurance programs usually provide for two types of benefits: replacement of earnings lost due to disability and payment of the costs of medical care.

Previous chapters have discussed cash benefits for total and permanent disability under OASDI and the public assistance program of aid to the needy permanently and totally disabled. This latter program of public assistance to the disabled also provides medical care services.

This chapter will discuss the various governmental and voluntary programs in the United States (other than OASDI and public assistance) which provide cash benefits to replace lost earnings due to disability and to pay the costs of medical care.

The greatest hazard for the average worker is sickness. In the United States, on an average day, more than two million persons are absent from work because of temporary disability, resulting in many millions of dollars of lost wages and earnings and additional sums to pay the costs of the illness. Private expenditures alone for medical care were $19.6 billion in 1960. About $13.7 billion was spent by consumers directly to medical vendors and the remainder consisted of expenditures for insurance and prepayment plans. In addition to direct expenditures, the income loss to wage workers and salary workers is approximately $7.5 billion annually.

Almost every worker either experiences illness himself or experiences the effects of illness in some member of his family or close friend or relative. For the worker, temporary disability or sickness means not only the loss of income but additional expenses caused by the illness. There is, therefore, a double blow to the economic security of the worker when he is temporarily ill. In dealing with temporary illness, therefore, we are involved in considering a factor whose impact upon the economy is a strong one.

The risk of temporary disability is a measurable risk.[130] Because the extent and cost of temporary illness can be ascertained with some degree of accuracy, a large voluntary insurance program has grown up in the United States and there has also developed the beginnings of limited public social insurance programs similar to the programs of Europe. These programs cover both temporary and permanent disability.

Sickness disability insurance is a basic form of social insurance in European countries and in many other countries throughout the world, and was one of the first forms of social insurance to receive widespread recognition and adoption. Stemming from the voluntary efforts of workers themselves in a variety of workers' guilds and fraternal orders, sickness insurance became firmly established as part of the social insurance program. Although many countries had developed a variety of sickness benefits on both a voluntary and governmental basis prior to the compulsory sickness act in Germany of 1893, that was the first comprehensive governmental health insurance program. It was later expanded to include most of the population of the country. The German program served as a model for other countries and stimulated the growth of sickness insurance. Several countries established sickness insurance during the next thirty years.[131]

In contradistinction to the influence of the German and British systems on United States programs of old-age, survivors, and disability insurance, unemployment insurance, and workmen's compensation, the temporary disability insurance programs of foreign countries had little effect on the United States. This was due to a variety of reasons. Perhaps the most important reason was the growth of voluntary insurance to cover temporary illness at a time when the United States was beginning to develop its social insurance program to cover other risks. (See Table VIII, Appendix.)

There was a flurry of national interest in a health insurance program prior to 1920 and again in 1938. The interest generated, however, soon died down because of the combined opposition of the medical profession, the commercial insurance companies, and employer groups.

It is probably correct to say that the lack of a comprehensive program of health insurance in the United States is due to three factors: (1) the rapid growth of voluntary health insurance both through nonprofit organizations and commercial insurance companies; (2) the strong opposition of the medical profession, employer associations, and insurance companies; (3) the growth of a variety of medical care programs which eased the impact and shock of illness—such as veterans' programs, labor union medical programs, employer-financed medical programs, publicly supported hospitals for the indigent, and medical care programs for public assistance recipients.

In spite of the lack of a comprehensive social insurance program covering temporary disability insurance, the vast majority of America's workers have some protection against the hazards of temporary illness. This protection is of two types: voluntary insurance and social insurance.

Voluntary Insurance. Voluntary insurance covering temporary sickness has grown rapidly. In 1939, less than eight million persons had voluntary insurance coverage. Twenty years later, in 1959, almost 128 million, or nearly three-quarters of the population, had some type of prepaid insurance protection.[132] Voluntary insurance is available through nonprofit plans or commercial insurance companies.

The increasing cost of hospitalization and medical care gave rise to a variety of nonprofit plans to cover such hospital and medical costs. Sponsored by hospitals and medical societies, they have grown rapidly. For example, in 1940, only 63 persons out of every thousand had hospitalization coverage through nonprofit plans. In 1959, 350 persons out of every thousand had hospitalization coverage under such nonprofit plans. Nonprofit plans include those established by fraternal orders, employer plans, union plans, and physician-operated plans; however, most persons are covered by plans that are known as Blue Cross.

The Blue Cross plans in the United States cover almost fifty-four million persons for hospital expenses (Table VIII, Appendix). The

Blue Cross plan is very simple. Usually the hospitals in a certain area organize a nonprofit corporation and enroll persons (primarily in groups) who pay a monthly premium; the funds collected are paid to the member hospitals on the basis of agreed-upon fees among the hospital members of the group Blue Cross plan when such hospitals furnish care to the individual person enrolled. Persons usually join such Blue Cross plans as part of an employee group. Many plans accept individual members.

A "Blue Shield" plan is organized in the same manner as Blue Cross and frequently is operated by the same over-all organization. Blue Shield usually provides—in addition to hospitalization and related medical care in the hospital, which is provided by Blue Cross —surgical treatments and, in certain instances, some physician's care in the home and office. Benefits are provided on the basis of the service rendered. In 1959, 116,944,000 persons had some type of surgical insurance, representing approximately two-thirds of the entire population.

Medical insurance covering care of patients and medical costs outside of the hospital are not as well covered by insurance as hospitalization and surgical insurance coverage. In 1959, 82,615,000 persons had some type of medical insurance coverage.

Individual private commercial insurance companies began to develop extensive commercial insurance plans during the depression of the 1930's. Many of these companies operate on a nonprofit basis since they are mutual companies. However, the large growth of these plans has come about since the end of World War II. These plans usually provide hospital benefits, medical and surgical benefits, and replacement of income lost. Most of the hospital insurance coverage written involves group plans; that is, the person is insured through a group, usually at his place of employment. However, increasingly such group plans are being developed for professional associations, fraternal orders, churches, and other such groups. The insurance companies generally pay cash benefits to the insured persons. The patient pays the difference between the amount covered under the insurance policy and the charge of the hospital.

The estimated loss of income from sickness and disability to wage and salary workers in 1960 was $8.6 billion.[133] Of this loss, approximately $1 billion is returned in cash benefits from insurance policies. Protection against loss of earnings during periods of short-term sickness is provided in several ways. Voluntary protection may be provided through group or individual accident and sickness insurance policies sold by commercial carriers. Employers may also self-insure, providing either cash benefits or paid sick leave. A variety of union, employer, fraternal societies, and mutual benefit associations have cash disability benefit plans. A substantial percentage of the income loss for short-term sickness is covered by established sick leave plans. In 1960, workers covered by sick leave plans had an income loss of $1.4 billion, but the value of sick leave was $1 billion; covering 72 per cent of the loss. In addition, there is a considerable amount of continuation of salary by employers on an informal basis (e.g., among small employers).

During the 1930's there was considerable agitation to establish a social insurance program covering wage loss resulting from temporary disability or short-term sickness. Four states established such programs under state law. Rhode Island established its program in 1942, California in 1946, New Jersey in 1948, and New York in 1949. These four state plans plus the temporary disability program for railroad workers constitute the five public plans in the United States covering temporary disability. There are, however, a number of additional plans for employees of governmental agencies. It is estimated that about eleven million workers, or more than one-fifth of the regularly employed wage and salary workers, are covered by the five existing temporary disability programs.

Types of Plans. The five plans mentioned reflect three different approaches to the problem of insuring workers against wage loss when they are unable to work because of temporary disability. Each plan provides weekly cash payments for temporary disability.[134] The California program provides hospital benefits (in addition to weekly cash benefits) of $12 a day for twenty days in a benefit period. In Rhode Island (also under the Railroad Unemployment Insurance Act) all employers must insure their workers for temporary disability through a publicly operated insurance fund into which all contributions are deposited and from which all benefits are paid. The programs are closely allied with unemployment insurance, in that the same group of workers is covered, the same type of qualifying conditions are used, and the same wages and credits serve as a basis for contributions and benefits. Some employers provide supplemental benefits. However, this is not required by law.

In California and New Jersey, employers may insure with a state fund or may insure with a private fund; that is, they may purchase insurance from commercial carriers. Employers may also self-insure; however, the private plan must be approved by the state as a substitute for the state plan. Until such approval, workers are automatically covered by the state temporary disability insurance fund. The law provides that the premium paid by the worker under the private plan may not be any greater than the contribution he would be required to pay to the state fund.

The New York program is entirely different from that of the other three states. It is completely separate from unemployment insurance and is administered by the State Workmen's Compensation Board. Insurance is carried primarily through state-approved private plans. The payment of benefits to workers who become sick is made by the private insurance companies. The state does, however, administer a special fund to finance benefits when disability commences after the fourth week of unemployment or when the employer has failed to carry the required insurance.

There has been considerable agitation for extension of publicly established social insurance programs for temporary illness. President Kennedy has recommended that persons aged 65 and over eligible to receive benefits under old-age, survivors, and disability insurance and Railroad Retirement be covered for hospitalization costs during disability or illness. Labor unions, in the past, have asked for a comprehensive health insurance plan tied to Social Security, and a number of groups have been pressing for state legislation similar to the programs in operation in the four states.

Probably the most important factor hampering the expansion of the public programs of cash and medical care benefits through temporary disability insurance to states other than the four mentioned is the issue of public versus private insurance. Many persons believe that the New York plan does not provide the necessary controls over standards that are required to make the plan effective. On the other hand, persons favoring the New York plan oppose a monopolistic state fund, such as is found in Rhode Island, and even oppose the California type of program, which provides for setting of standards by the state. Private insurers claim that they can administer the program more efficiently than government agencies. On the other hand, persons favoring competitive or monopolistic state funds feel that either a yardstick is essential through a competitive state fund, or a publicly controlled fund is necessary to be sure that benefits and contributions bear a close relationship to each other without permitting excessive profits.

Viewing the protection afforded the American people by the combination of the publicly established social insurance plans and the private plans previously mentioned, there are two opposing points of view. Many persons feel that the coverage of the American people today is far superior to coverage of some countries with a longer history of insuring against disabling illness; on the other hand, many feel that coverage is only partial in terms of the numbers covered, that benefits are small in relationship to total expenditures, and that the next step must be a publicly established social insurance program, which insures against the risk of temporary and permanent illness and disability in the same way that old-age, survivors, and disability insurance insures against the risks of old age, death, and total and permanent disability.

"Oh, farewell, honest soldier." [135] —*Shakespeare*

CHAPTER XIII

VETERANS' BENEFITS

In the wars of the United States the American military man has been primarily a civilian who returned to civil life upon completion of his military service. Some returned disabled, some at a disadvantage because of economic loss by reason of absence from civilian employment, a few died in the service of their country. In recognition of such service the United States has, from the beginning of its history, provided a variety of veterans' benefits. Such veterans' benefits have particular significance today since the two World Wars and the Korean conflict have resulted in a large veteran population. Of the 180 million Americans, eighty-one million are living veterans, members of families of living veterans, or dependent survivors. These veterans and their families constitute 45 per cent of the population of the United States.[136]

Veterans' benefits and services for these veterans and their families are available through the Veterans Administration of the United States Government and through a variety of state programs. Their significance may be grasped by the fact that in 1960 the expenditures of the Veterans Administration alone constituted 7 per cent of the total expenditures of the United States Government and exceeded $6.4 billion.

Special benefits to persons who have served in the military forces of their country have been provided by nations almost since the dawn of recorded history. The United States, likewise, has made provision for special benefits for veterans and their dependents through a variety of programs. Special assistance to wounded veterans was provided in the colonies even before the United States became a nation.

The first national pension law was enacted on August 26, 1776, by the Continental Congress.[137] It provided for half-pay for life to anyone unable to work by reason of disabilities incurred while in the armed forces. A partial pension was provided for those partially disabled. However, the operation and financing of the pension program was left to the states, so that its administration was not uniform. With the establishment of the Federal Government in 1789, the administration of the pension program was centralized and the United States Government took over the payment of the Revolutionary War pensions.[138] With this beginning, the United States initiated a program of veterans' pensions which has continued to expand until the present time.

Until World War I, the veterans' benefits consisted mainly of retirement pay, land grants, service pensions, and domiciliary care. Medical care was available to residents in the National Homes established for disabled soldiers, later known as domiciliaries. In 1917, the United States developed new legislation to provide financial support for dependents of servicemen, low-cost insurance, medical care and rehabilitation, as well as service-connected disability and death benefits. Congress created the Veterans Bureau in 1921 and then authorized it a year later to make its hospital facilities available to all veterans of the Spanish-American War who suffered from "neuropsychiatric and tubercular ailments and diseases." In 1924, hospital treatment was extended to all veterans so far as hospital facilities would permit. In 1930, the Veterans Administration was created in a reorganization move by Congress to combine into one agency the responsibility for administering veterans' programs previously shared by a number of bureaus and agencies.

The huge program of veterans' benefits is carried on primarily by the Veterans Administration (VA), headed by an Administrator of Veterans Affairs, appointed by the President, with the advice and consent of the Senate. The agency has 172,000 employees who are responsible for the expenditure of over $6 billion annually.

The original philosophy of veterans' benefits was based upon the concept that the government should express its gratitude to those who served it well and should prevent men who were in military service from becoming indigents. As a result, a number of pension programs were established and modified over the years. Following World War II, greater emphasis was placed upon helping the veteran adjust to civilian life after his military experience and upon assisting him to make up the loss in his economic advancement due to military service. The major emphasis has been to put the veteran back into normal employment without undue hardship. This was done through many laws, the chief one being the Servicemen's Readjustment Act of 1944—frequently referred to as the G.I. Bill of Rights.

The major veterans' benefits and services can be grouped in three categories: medical care and treatment, government life insurance, and financial assistance to veterans and dependents of deceased veterans.

The medical care program is provided through the largest organized medical system in the nation: 171 hospitals, 93 outpatient clinics, and 18 domiciliaries. The system also uses non-VA hospitals, state homes, and private practitioners in areas where VA facilities are not available. There are 120,500 beds in operation for daily care of veterans in the VA hospitals.

In an annnual sample census taken of all VA patients on October 31, 1959, it was found that there were 114,400 patients hospitalized. The largest group of these (58.6 per cent) were veterans who did not have a compensable service-connected disability and who signed an affidavit that they were unable to defray the cost of hospitalization. The majority of these were patients with long-term illness or receiving care for disabilities which are classified as chronic. In 1960, a total of 547,000 patients was admitted. There were more than 3-1/2 million medical visits for outpatient care.

Veterans are admitted to veterans hospitals on a priority basis. The first priority is for those needing hospitalization because of injuries or diseases incurred or aggravated in line of duty in active service during any war. A second priority goes to those with service during any war who were discharged or retired for disability incurred in line of duty or who are receiving compensation or would be eligible to receive compensation except for the receipt of retirement pay for service-connected disabilities, but who need treatment for some ailment not connected with their service. Such persons will be admitted as a second priority if beds are available. The third priority is for those other veterans with war service who meet the following conditions: (a) hospitalization is necessary;

(b) they are financially unable to pay hospital charges; and (c) beds are available.

If a veteran is admitted to a veterans hospital, he receives complete care. Outpatient care is limited to veterans with service-connected disabilities, except for veterans of the Spanish-American War.

Veterans who served only during peacetime are eligible for hospital care with similar admission priorities if they meet the same conditions as the service-connected group above. Priority goes to those needing hospitalization because of injuries or diseases incurred or aggravated in the line of duty in active service.

The second large veterans' program is government insurance, which is administered through two large life insurance plans for the benefit of servicemen, veterans, and their beneficiaries. The World War I program provides both a death benefit and a permanent total disability benefit without terminal age, which matures the policy and pays the face value and interest in installments over twenty years, or for life if disability continues. The World War II program provides a death benefit and a total disability premium waiver benefit terminating at age 60. An optional total disability monthly benefit is available at extra cost to the insured. The maximum on all government life insurance is $10,000. The size of the program places it as one of the largest insurance programs in the world.

The financial assistance and compensation programs and services are varied and complex. They include financial assistance for education and training, pensions for disability, loans, and a variety of other assistance plans.

Education and Training. Large numbers of veterans of World War II and the Korean conflict received education and training at government expense.[139] The major G.I. Bill of Rights for World War II veterans ended July 25, 1956. Under this program, 7.8 million veterans received education and training by June 30, 1960. Approximately 30 per cent attended colleges or universities. Training could be paid for up to four years, depending upon length of service. In addition to tuition and training expenses, the veteran received a subsistence allowance of $75 a month for a veteran without dependents, $105 with one dependent, and $120 with two or more dependents. Veterans of the Korean conflict are also entitled to education benefits, and this readjustment program is predominantly a college program.

War Orphans Education Assistance. Children of veterans of the Spanish-American War, World War I, World War II, Korean conflict, and induction periods following September 16, 1940, between the ages of 18 and 23, whose parent died from disease or injury incurred or aggravated in the line of duty in active service, are eligible for assistance to complete their education. They may receive as much as thirty-six months of educational assistance. In the year ending June 30, 1960, which was the fourth year of the program, 41,800 war orphans had applied for assistance. Young men and women in school under this program receive $110 per month if enrolled full time.

Compensation for Service-Connected Disabilities. Veterans who are disabled by injury or disease incurred in or aggravated by active service in line of duty either during wartime or peacetime service are entitled to monthly payments in amounts that depend on the severity of the disability, but not to exceed $600. Disabilities are rated according to a schedule and the monthly compensation is based on the percentage of disability. For example, if a person is only 10 per cent disabled from war-connected disabilities, he would receive $19; if 50 per cent disabled, he would receive $100. The usual monthly rates of compensation for war-connected disabilities vary from $19 per month to $225 per month depending on the degree of disability. (Figure 7 below.)

Figure 7

Monthly Compensation Rates for Wartime Service-Connected Disabilities

Disability of	Monthly Compensation
10 per cent	$ 19.00
20 per cent	36.00
30 per cent	55.00
40 per cent	73.00
50 per cent	100.00
60 per cent	120.00
70 per cent	140.00
80 per cent	160.00
90 per cent	225.00
Total Disability	(For special circumstances may go up to $600)

Specific disabilities may bring higher payments. Veterans whose service-connected disabilities are rated at 50 per cent or more are entitled to additional allowance for dependents. (Figure 8 below.)

Figure 8

Selected Veterans' Dependents' Benefits for 100 per cent Wartime Service-Connected Disability (for less than 100 per cent disability a percentage reduction applies)

Dependents	Monthly Allowance
Wife only	$23.00
Wife and 1 child	39.00
Wife and 2 children	50.00
Wife and 3 children	62.00
Each additional child	12.00
One parent	19.00
Two parents	38.00

Veterans of service in the armed forces during peacetime may be eligible for disability compensation. They then are entitled to monthly payments of 80 per cent of the wartime rates. If their disability is more than 50 per cent, they may receive additional dependents allowances.

Pensions for Nonservice-Connected Disabilities. Veterans of World War I, World War II, and the Korean conflict who are permanently and totally disabled from conditions not connected with military service may receive pensions under specified conditions. Spanish-American War veterans are eligible for a service pension; for ninety days or more of service or disability discharge the monthly rate is $101.59; those with seventy days of service receive $67.73. Pensions are payable also to veterans of the two World Wars and the Korean conflict, who are permanently and totally disabled and have had ninety days of service. The veteran's annual income must be below $1,400 if he is unmarried or $2,700 if he is married or if he has a minor child.

Beginning July 1, 1960, a new pension law became effective.[140] Under the old system, the monthly rate is $66.15, and this amount is increased to $78.75 after continuous receipt of a pension for ten years, or after continuous disability, or upon attainment of age 65. For veterans who are bedridden or blind or who require the aid and attendance of another person the rate is $135.45. Veterans on the rolls on June 30, 1960, and receiving pensions under the old system, have the right to remain on the old system or to choose instead the new system. Once this choice is made, however, it cannot be changed again. All veterans who come on the pension rolls on or after July 1, 1960, will have no choice of the old system but will receive pensions under the new system.

A major difference in the new system is related to other income. Under the new law, the less income a veteran has the more pension he will draw; the more income a veteran has the less monthly pension he will draw. A veteran with no dependents who has income over $1,800 per year is not eligible for any pension payment. If the annual income is under $1,800, then the pension will vary from $40 per month to $85 per month. A veteran with a wife or dependent child who has income over $3,000 is not eligible for a pension. Income of his wife above $1,200 a year (except in hardship cases) is included in the income count. The pension payment varies from $45 to $100 a month. As of June 30, 1960, 947,250 veterans were receiving pensions for nonservice-connected disabilities.[141]

Compensation for Service-Connected Deaths, and Pensions for Nonservice-Connected Deaths. Compensation is payable to dependents and survivors of veterans, *i.e.*, their widows, children, and dependent parents.

On January 1, 1957, a new law became effective. This new law provides for payments, called dependency and indemnity compensation, for service-connected death; the payments are intended to replace death compensation and servicemen's indemnity (insurance) payments. Survivors of veterans who died from service-connected causes prior to January 1, 1957, may elect to receive compensation under the new law. Death compensation established prior to that date continues in effect for survivors who have not elected compensation payments under the terms of the new law, and the compensation rates provided under the old system apply in those cases. The awards vary in amount. For example, the widow of a veteran who died from causes connected with his service would receive a dependents and indemnity compensation award of $112 per month plus 12 per cent of his basic pay but under no conditions less than a minimum of $122. In addition, the relatives of a person who dies in service are entitled to six months' pay from the Armed Forces in an amount not less than $800 nor more than $3,000. As of June 30, 1960, 561,000 persons were receiving compensation under either the old or the new law on the basis of the death of a veteran while in service or from service-connected causes.

Pensions are paid to certain unremarried widows and children of veterans of World War I, World War II, and the Korean conflict who died of nonservice-connected causes if their income is below $1,400 annually for a widow alone and $2,700 annually for a widow with children. Such survivors would receive pensions which generally are $50.40 per month for the widow, $63 for a widow with a child, plus $7.56 for each additional child.

Beginning July 1, 1960, the new pension law changed the benefits applicable to widows and children. A widow without children may receive from $25 to $60 monthly depending on her income (over $1,800—no payment). A widow with children is entitled to $15 additional for each child and the income limitation in these cases is $3,000 annually.

Unemployment Compensation. The Veterans Readjustment Assistance Act of 1952 provides unemployment compensation for veterans with military service on or after June 27, 1950. Benefits are paid by the state employment security agencies through the same procedures applicable to unemployment insurance under the Social Security Act. The benefits, depending upon the laws of the various states, range from $26 per week up to $55. In a few states, additional amounts are payable for dependents. The maximum period for which weekly benefits are payable ranges in various states from twenty to thirty-nine weeks.

Automobiles and Other Conveyances. Certain specifically disabled veterans (of World War II and the Korean conflict) who need special automobiles or other types of conveyances, such as motorized wheel chairs, may receive up to $1,600 toward the cost of such conveyances. At present, over 46,000 veterans have been assisted in the purchase of such conveyances.

Vocational Rehabilitation. Veterans of World War II and the Korean conflict who have disabilities incurred or aggravated in service are provided vocational rehabilitation services by the Veterans Administration to meet their individual needs. This vocational rehabilitation service starts with comprehensive vocational counselling to assist them in assessing their interests, aptitudes, and abilities, in choosing a suitable occupational goal, and in developing their vocational rehabilitation plans. Assistance of counsellors and rehabilitation specialists is continued as needed to locate suitable training facilities, and throughout the period of training and adjustment in employment. While in training and for two months after rehabilitation, eligible disabled veterans may receive a subsistence allowance in addition to their disability compensation. Basic monthly subsistence rates for the disabled veteran enrolled full-time in school is $75 without dependents, $105 with one dependent, and $120 with more than one dependent. Basic rates for on-the-job training are $65 without dependents and $90 with one or more dependents.

Loans for Homes, Farms, Businesses. Veterans and some widows of veterans of World War II and the Korean conflict may qualify for certain Veterans Administration guaranteed or insured loans for the following three purposes: (a) to purchase, construct, or improve a home; (b) to buy a farm, stock, feed, and seed, farm machinery, and other farm supplies and equipment; and (c) to buy a business or otherwise to enable a veteran to undertake or expand a business venture. Any lender making a G.I. home loan is guaranteed against loss up to 60 per cent of the loan with a maximum guarantee of $7,500. Interest rates on such guaranteed loans may not exceed 5-1/4 per cent per year on the unpaid balance.

The repayment period of G.I. home loans may be as long as thirty years. The length of time within which veterans may obtain G.I. loans depends on their date of discharge from their last period of active wartime duty and the number of months of active wartime service, *i.e.,* ten years from date of discharge plus one year for each three months of active wartime service. However, no World War II veteran's entitlement expired prior to July 25, 1962, nor extends beyond July 25, 1967. The delimiting dates for Korean veterans are July 25, 1965, and July 25, 1975.

Direct Loans. The Veterans Administration is authorized to make direct loans up to $15,000 to eligible veterans to construct or purchase a home, to purchase a farm on which there is a farm residence, or to repair, alter, or improve a farm residence or other dwelling to be occupied as his home.[142] Under this program, the Veterans Administration has made 165,000 direct loans to veterans in an amount exceeding $1-1/3 billion. These loans are made to veterans only in areas where the Administrator has determined that guaranteed loan financing has not been generally available.

Wheelchair Homes. Grants are also available to certain service-connected disabled veterans for specially adapted housing where their disability requires it. Approximately six thousand grants have been made for such housing. These grants may be made in an amount up to $10,000 for each veteran.

Other Programs for Veterans. Other agencies have specialized programs to assist veterans also. Both Federal and state civil service programs give preference in employment to veterans. Every state has established some type of veterans' benefit or assistance program. Most of the states have state departments or agencies which administer a variety of benefit and loan programs or special assistance programs for needy veterans. Some states have established institutions for the care of veterans. In addition, many states provide funds to veterans' organizations to enable them to establish offices to represent veterans in connection with their claims before state veterans' organizations and Veterans Administration officials.

Military Pensions. For career personnel in the armed forces, a liberal noncontributory retirement plan is provided after twenty years of service. The maximum retirement amount is 75 per cent of the base pay immediately prior to retirement. In addition, persons in the armed forces are covered under OASDI. The OASDI payments, which, of course, are the same as OASDI benefits paid to all other beneficiaries, are in addition to payments from the armed forces retirement program. Members of the armed forces also have comprehensive disability pension programs.

"When men are employed, they are best contented." [148] —
Benjamin Franklin

CHAPTER XIV

EMPLOYEE BENEFIT AND RETIREMENT PLANS

During the past twenty years there has been a tremendous growth in various employee benefit plans, so that today more than 130 million persons (including dependents of workers) are covered by some "employee benefit" such as hospitalization, life insurance, retirement pensions, sickness insurance, and a variety of other employee benefits. These "employee benefit" plans may be established by an individual firm or business or they may be industry-wide plans. In either case they may be established on the initiative of the employer or employers or through collective bargaining with labor unions. The widespread coverage of these plans is indicated in Table IX (Appendix).

Although employee benefit plans have many gaps in coverage, they do constitute an important aspect of the total economic security picture supplementing and complementing the social security program. It is estimated that various "fringe benefits," i.e., benefits other than straight salaries and wages, cost over 26 per cent of payroll in those industries and businesses employing the vast majority of American workers. Employers and employees paid $12.3 billion in 1960 as contributions for such employee benefits (employers pay about 75 per cent of the total contributions), and in 1960 employees received approximately $7.8 billion in benefits (the remainder going into reserves in respect of future benefits).

Pension and retirement plans are the largest of the fringe benefits in terms of cost. In 1960, they accounted for 43 per cent of the total contributions in respect of all employee benefit plans. Both employers and labor unions have established retirement plans. Some plans are entirely employer sponsored; in these plans the employer establishes the plan on his own initiative and usually pays the entire cost, while in other cases the employees pay part of the cost.

The first industrial pension plan established by an employer was that of the American Express Company in 1875.[144] By 1935, when the Social Security Act was enacted, pension plans had been established by some individual firms in most of the industries in the country although coverage was limited to a very small group. Labor unions, likewise, have a long history of union-sponsored retirement and pension plans. Probably the first plan was that of the Pattern Makers' League of North America in 1900. Although many unions established such plans in the succeeding years, the establishment of union plans was slow, particularly after collective bargaining efforts brought employer-employee negotiated plans into existence in great numbers.

A number of theories have been formulated to justify private pension programs in industry. One concept is that of "human depreciation." Under this concept, it is believed that industry owes an obligation to workers to provide benefits to take care of the depreciation of the individual in the form of old-age retirement in the same way that it does for depreciation of plants and machinery.[145] In spite of the fact that this has been widely accepted, it does not appear to be based on any logical principles. Aging is a physiological process and is not necessarily connected with employment. In many cases, aging is not accelerated by employment and may actually be postponed because of the mental and physical advantages of particular types of employment. Another theory that has been advanced is that of deferred wages. Employers and employees together have the choice of having additional wages paid now or deferring them into a retirement plan. This theory has had considerable vogue and a long history, and it was expressed by a student of the problem as early as 1913.[146]

Frequently, the justification for industrial pensions has been put forth on the theory of increased production. This theory emphasizes that an industrial pension plan will result in increased production—first because the security given to the individual makes him a better employee and encourages him to work harder for the company; and second, by retiring superannuated workers whose productivity has decreased, the total production of the company is raised. Others have urged that an industrial pension plan is one way of retaining competent workers. Such workers find it difficult to leave after many years of service because of the investment in the retirement plan. Some personnel directors of large companies have emphasized that the industrial pension plan provides for a way of retiring older workers and making way for younger workers, thus developing good morale among younger workers because of the opportunities for promotion. As for labor unions, their own plans have been developed because of the desire of their own members for greater economic security in old age.

Whatever the rationale given, there is no doubt that industrial pensions have been developed for a variety of reasons, including certain tax inducements offered to employers by the Federal Government in connection with income tax. An employer may deduct his contributions to a pension plan as an operating expense of business, providing the plan meets certain conditions established by Federal law.

There are so many different plans and so many different patterns that it is difficult to make generalizations with reference to them. Although the more than twenty-five thousand plans in existence vary considerably, they have certain common general characteristics. They provide retirement benefits at a certain age; the benefits are either flat benefits based on length of service, or wage-related benefits, or a combination of both; if the employee leaves the job, he usually receives all of the contributions he may have made; increasingly, plans provide for his receiving the benefit of the employer contributions in the form of a vested deferred pension if he does not withdraw any contributions he may have made; most employees are covered under plans which directly or indirectly relate benefit levels to take account of those received under old-age, survivors, and disability insurance.

Retirement plans have been classified into two types: "pattern" plans and "conventional" plans. The pattern plans provide a flat pension not related to wages but frequently based on length of service. Under this type of plan, for example, a worker with twenty years of service who reaches the retirement age with average earnings during the twenty years of service of $200 per month would receive the same benefit as the worker in exactly the same circumstances who earned $400 per month. The conventional plan is usually related to average wage and length of service. The higher the wage, the greater the benefit; and the benefit increases with length of service.

Age and service requirements govern entrance into some pension plans and determine eligibility to benefits. Many plans have both minimum and maximum age limits. The minimum age limit at which a person can enter the plan is usually 25 to 30 years of age. The reason for such a minimum age requirement is to protect the plan from a large number of drop-outs, since younger workers are very mobile and leave employment frequently. The trend is in the direction of eliminating this minimum age requirement. Maximum age requirements for entrance into the plan are usually 55 to 60. The purpose is to enable the employee to work the minimum years of service to qualify before reaching retirement age.

In order to retire and receive benefits, the worker usually must have attained the "normal" retirement age. Under most plans, this age is 65. Some plans provide lower retirement ages for women. During the past few years, there has been no appreciable trend toward retirement age reduction for the normal retirement or full retirement benefit. There has, however, been a trend to reduce the number of required years of service. Most plans permit retirement prior to the normal retirement age and also permit workers to continue working after that age if the worker wishes and the employer approves. Such retirement before the normal retirement age is generally with reduced benefits and is usually available after ten to fifteen years of service and the attainment of a certain age, usually 55 or 60.

The retirement benefit is computed differently under different bases. There are three general bases: those where benefits are related to past earnings and years of service; those related to service only; and flat benefits for those who meet service requirements.

Under the first basis, the benefit is based on a percentage of pay for each year of service. Many of the plans use a final pay period or highest pay period; *i.e.*, the pay used will be the highest for five or ten years of the employee's service. Other plans consider total compensation or, in other words, average salary over the entire period of service. Frequently, a lower percentage is applied to the first part of a salary, for example, the first $3,000 (so as to recognize the presence of the "weighted" old-age, survivors, and disability insurance benefits).

The second basis relates to length of service only. Under this method, the benefit is a flat dollar amount for each year of service, with possibly a maximum number of years of service creditable.

The third type of formula provides a flat uniform benefit after a specified period of service, for example, $100 a month after twenty-five years of service, with no benefits for shorter service.

The trend is in the direction of the first type. This method, based on average or highest earnings and length of service, is generally found in retirement programs for government employees also.

Benefit levels have been increasing over the past several years. The trend has been to raise the minimum and maximum benefits and to have them computed independently of old-age benefits under old-age, survivors, and disability insurance (although recognizing its presence in setting the benefit level). Growing also is the number of plans which provide cost of living increases. Total benefit disbursements in 1960 were 4-1/2 times as large as in 1950, whereas the number of pensioners was about four times as large, indicating an increase in average benefits. The major plans, when added to old-age benefits under the Social Security Act, generally provide a maximum of from one-half to three-fourths of the average monthly wage.

Until the past twelve years, the administration of the plans was usually handled exclusively by the employer. Increasingly, employees are represented in the administration of such pension plans. The majority of persons covered by pension plans are in plans financed exclusively by the employer. In 1960, employers contributed about 85 per cent of the cost of retirement plans and employees about 15 per cent of the cost. The funds collected are paid either to insurance companies, which pay the benefits on the basis of either individual employee or group employee contracts (called "insured plans"), or into noninsured plans operated by trustees. The majority of plans are insured. However, they are usually the plans of smaller companies and cover only about one-fourth of the employees. Three-fourths of the employees are covered by the noninsured plans. The contributions are placed in a "trust" (usually a bank), which invests the funds and pays out the benefits. The trend is in the direction of having an increasingly larger percentage of employees covered under noninsured plans.

In the early plans, an employee acquired no rights to the employer's contributions until he was eligible for retirement. If he left the job prior to retirement, he could withdraw or receive benefits only from his own contributions, if any. However, a trend has developed in the direction of "vesting." This refers to the right of the employee to terminate his employment and still obtain the accrued pension resulting from the employer's contributions. This may take the form of an early retirement and payment of a reduced pension immediately, a deferred pension which is payable at a certain age, or (rarely) immediate cash payment including all or a portion of the employer's contributions. The trend toward vesting is indicated by the fact that in 1959, 82 per cent of the pattern plans had some type of vesting for employees satisfying certain age and/or service requirements at separation, compared with 33 per cent in 1952; the conventional plans had vesting provisions in 90 per cent of the plans in 1959 compared with 75 per cent of the plans in 1952.[147]

In summary, private retirement plans are increasing, bringing added economic security to about twenty-two million workers. These plans paid out $1.7 billion in retirement benefits in 1960. There is little doubt that the trend will continue both in terms of covering more workers and in terms of increased benefit outgo. The development of private retirement plans has been spotty and unco-ordinated and there are great gaps in coverage. For those people who are covered, however, they do provide desirable supplemental retirement benefits to old-age, survivors, and disability insurance, and are an important source of additional security for the retired worker.

"Laying up in store for themselves a good foundation against the time to come." [148] —*I. Timothy*

CHAPTER XV

Voluntary Life Insurance, Savings, and Home Ownership

The social security program of the United States has been developing during a period when the standard of living has been rising significantly for the large majority of the American people. Such social security program is influenced by the fact that most Americans have a variety of real and personal property resources. Americans own three-fourths of all the passenger automobiles in the world —approximately one for each American family. Ownership of land is likewise widespread.

Three of the more important resources contributing to economic security of the people in the United States are voluntary life insurance, savings, and home ownership.

Life insurance plays an important role in the economic security of the American people and represents a major source of income to families upon the death of the insured. At the end of 1960, about 118 million Americans, or approximately 65 per cent of all persons in the United States, owned life insurance.[149] The average amount of life insurance per family in 1960 was $10,200, but the average for the insured family was $12,800. In terms of average income, this latter amount was equivalent to twenty-five months of income. The tremendous growth of life insurance in the past decade is indicated by the fact that in 1950, just ten years earlier, the average life insurance per family was $4,600—less than half of the amount in force in 1960. In 1960, life insurance companies paid out $10.7 billion in benefit payments. About $8.1 billion was paid under life insurance and annuity contracts and $2.6 billion under health insurance policies. This amount of $2.6 billion is not the total paid out in health insurance payments by all insuring organizations but only the total paid out by life insurance companies.

This large American insurance industry has a long history. The first life insurance company in the United States was established in 1759 in Philadelphia. Established by the Synod of the Presbyterian Church, it was called "The Corporation for Relief of Poor and Distressed Presbyterian Ministers and of the Poor and Distressed Widows and Children of Presbyterian Ministers." This company, now the Presbyterian Ministers' Fund, is the oldest life insurance company in continued existence in the world. In 1794, the Insurance Company of North America was chartered as the first general insurance company to sell life insurance. The legal reserve life insurance companies which write most of the insurance were in every state of the union in 1960 and totalled 1,455 separate companies. Twenty companies had been in business for over one hundred years. The aggregate income of United States life insurance companies in 1960 was $23 billion, derived principally from premiums and investment earnings.

Several types of life insurance programs or policies are in force in the United States. A significant amount is written by Canadian companies (only a small amount by other foreign companies). Likewise, United States companies write much business in Canada. The figures quoted here are related to all insurance carried by United States residents regardless of the domicile of the insurer.

Ordinary Life Insurance. Ordinary life insurance is the most important. It usually involves a contract between an individual and a life insurance company under which the individual makes regular premium payments and upon death the "face value" of the policy is paid to designated beneficiaries. Ordinary life insurance is usually issued in units of $1,000 or more and at the end of 1960 there were ninety-five million policies in force. The average-size ordinary life insurance policy was $3,590 in 1960; however, the average size of new ordinary life insurance policies purchased in 1960 was $6,050, indicating the increase in life insurance coverage.

Group Life Insurance. Group life insurance is a type of insurance which covers individuals in a group such as a factory, union, or association. At the end of 1960 about two-thirds of the nation's civilian, nonagricultural work force was covered by group insurance, and

43.5 million individual policies were in force under 169,000 group master contracts. The amount of family protection under group life insurance plans averaged about $4,030 per certificate at the close of 1960.

Industrial Life Insurance. Industrial life insurance is the descendant of the old worker's guilds insurance system. It is written in small amounts, usually under $1,000, and premiums are paid weekly or monthly. In 1960, there were one hundred million industrial policies in force, the average size being $390. This form has been gradually declining in importance.

Credit Life Insurance. Credit life insurance is written on the lives of borrowers and installment purchasers to cover loans in case of death. About 43.5 million individual policies and group certificates were in force at the end of 1960, with the average amount being $720.

Annuities. Annuities sold by life insurance companies provide income at such age as the individual policies provide. In 1960, about 1,345,000 persons were receiving annuity payments from United States life insurance companies, totalling $715 million per year. About 4.8 million persons were entitled to receive deferred annuities under outstanding annuity contracts.

More than half of all life insurance company benefit payments (totalling $8.1 billion in 1961) go to living policyholders in annuity payments, surrender values, policy dividends, matured endowments, and disability payments. In 1960, policyholders received a total of $4.8 billion.

A second major factor in assisting in the economic security of the American people is savings. The rise in personal income during the past several years has created an economic climate which is favorable for saving and investment by the American public. In 1960 an all-time record of $26.4 billion of personal income went into savings, which amounted to 7.5 per cent of total disposable income.[150] In total, net savings amounted to $235.2 billion in 1960, exclusive of investments of various kinds.

A third important resource contributing to economic security is home ownership. In 1960, home ownership reached the highest position in United States history. Sixty-two per cent of all nonfarm families own their own homes, as compared with 47 per cent in

1930. In all, over thirty-two million homes in our cities and nonfarm areas are now occupied by families or persons who are the home-owners.[151] Even in the lowest fifth of the population from the standpoint of income, almost half (46 per cent) of the families own their own homes.

The increase in home-owning families has constituted a significant trend in the economic life of American families. Home ownership increased from 47.8 per cent in 1890 to 61.9 per cent in 1960 and the trend is continuing because of a variety of reasons, such as higher income of the average American and government-sponsored low-cost financing programs.

The substantial resources indicated in the foregoing discussion of life insurance, savings, and home ownership are exclusive of the many billions of dollars invested in stocks of private corporations, government bonds other than savings bonds, and business investments of various kinds. Stock ownership alone constitutes a very significant financial asset. Over seventeen million persons own shares of stock in several thousand publicly held corporations. This is more than double the number of stockholders in 1952, which amounted to 6,490,000. These private resources are increasing—thereby increasing the economic security of the average American.

"Social security will always be a goal, never a finished thing, because human aspirations are infinitely expansible—just as human nature is infinitely perfectible." [152]—*Arthur J. Altmeyer*

CHAPTER XVI

SOCIAL SECURITY IN THE UNITED STATES—
WHAT LIES AHEAD?

In the previous chapters, the backgrounds and present status of various social security and related programs have been discussed. They constitute a large, complex, and significant group of governmental activities which are, today, firmly entrenched in our American social and political system and overwhelmingly supported by the American people. Like the social security programs of most countries, they have developed piecemeal—influenced by political, economic, and philosophical considerations, which have sometimes accelerated and sometimes retarded their development. One can point to numerous gaps in coverage, to low benefit payments, to weaknesses in financing of some parts of the total program, to local or state operation without effective Federal standards of some programs which are definitely in the area of Federal interest, to the complexity of the social security laws, to the illogical division of responsibility among the various levels of government for administration and financing—all these and more are serious problems, demanding the attention of the American people in the years ahead.

On the other hand, one can point to the rapid growth of the United States social security program—an expansion in twenty-seven years which has exceeded the expectations of most of its early supporters—a program which is making payments of more than $30 billion annually to approximately thirty million persons from public income maintenance programs alone, to which must be added several billion dollars from private pensions and private insurance; a program which is being improved and expanded with regularity by Congress and the states; a program which is bringing some measure of security to most of America's citizens.

As Arthur J. Altmeyer, the first Commissioner of Social Security, stated in the quotation at the beginning of this chapter, social security is "never a finished thing"—there remain many unfinished tasks and many questions which will be discussed and resolved in the years to come.[153] Still to be more clearly enunciated are the basic goals and objectives of America's social security program. Certainly a basic aim is the maintenance of a satisfactory level of well-being for the people in the United States.[154] Since we live in a money economy, this aim means the maintenance of sufficient income to attain a satisfactory level of well-being. How can this basic objective be achieved with minimum interference in the lives of our citizens and the orderly functioning of our economy? How can the programs promote rather than discourage individual initiative, economic independence, thrift, incentive, and individual self-sufficiency? With reference to this latter question as applied to the social insurances, social security officials maintain that "the old-age, survivors, and disability insurance program, like all our social insurance programs, is based on the concept that security for the individual should grow out of his own work. Under the old-age, survivors, and disability insurance program the worker earns his future security as he earns his living, and he pays toward the cost of his protection out of his earnings. Whether a worker is entitled to benefits, and the amount of his benefit and that of his family, is related to his own work. Basing eligibility on a demonstration of work and providing variable benefits related to the level of a worker's earnings reinforces the general system of economic incentives. Furthermore, since benefits are paid regardless of nonwork income from savings, pensions, investments, and the like, the worker is encouraged to supplement the basic protection afforded by his social insurance benefit with whatever additional protection he can afford to buy. Social insurance as a way of meeting need is a major social invention, largely eliminating the old fear that this will injure incentives to work and save." [155]

Because the United States uses both social insurance and social assistance programs, it has a framework within which all persons can be covered by social security. Social insurance has traditionally protected the gainfully employed and their dependents from the contingency of stoppage of income. Social assistance has protected those who are needy. Social assistance in the form of public assistance programs in the United States can protect all needy persons until social insurance expands to cover most of them. It can, and probably will, remain also a supplementary program, providing additional support to persons receiving social insurance payments in amounts insufficient for their needs.

Progress toward the goal of universal coverage of the entire population will involve the extension of old-age, survivors, and disability insurance, unemployment insurance, and workmen's compensation to all gainfully employed and their dependents, the abolition of all residence requirements for public assistance, and the abolition of all eligibility requirements for general assistance except that of need; in other words, all needy persons not otherwise cared for should be eligible for general assistance.

At this stage in the development of the United States social security system, these steps involve a relatively small expansion over the existing programs previously described. This accomplishment will not solve all of the problems of maintaining income, but almost universal coverage providing some protection could be achieved.

Another problem is the level or size of benefits under various programs. Benefit levels have risen in the past ten years. In April 1962 the average old-age benefit awarded to a retired worker in old-age, survivors, and disability insurance was $77.80, more than three times the amount of the average monthly payment of $25.11 awarded in 1945. Monthly family benefit amounts under old-age, survivors, and disability insurance increased even more; the average award for a widow with two children was $54.80 under the 1939 amendments in 1950 and $202.24 in 1960. Public assistance payments have shown increases also. An Old-Age Assistance recipient in December 1940 received an average monthly grant of $20.26; by April 1962, this had increased to $72.24. Aid to Families with Dependent Children's family payments rose from $32.38 per month in December 1940 to $123.92 in April 1962. The rise in average assistance payments is particularly significant because other income to assistance recipients has also risen, particularly from social insurance; and, in general, such increases in payments have risen faster than the cost of living.

Nevertheless, much needs to be done to bring the benefit levels into line with the aims previously expressed. They are still too low, and benefit levels in both the social insurance and public assistance programs will undoubtedly rise in the future.

Although most benefit payments under all types of social security programs are paid in cash, questions do arise as to whether benefits should be paid in cash or in kind in specific programs. In general, the United States is committed to cash payments for the social insurances except for medical care. In the assistance programs, cash benefits are generally paid and must be paid in the Federal categories. Some local communities pay assistance in kind in the general assistance program, *i.e.*, rent is paid to the landlord and grocery orders are given rather than cash. It seems quite certain that the principle of cash payments will continue to be the dominant method of payment for both social insurance and assistance.

Protection against the cost of medical care, both in social insurance (insofar as it exists) and in public and general assistance, is in the form of payment for services. There has been a strong movement to extend protection against the cost of medical care to aged persons eligible for old-age, survivors, and disability insurance benefits, and President Kennedy has recommended legislation to this effect.

A recurring question is one relating to the type of benefit. Should benefits be the same for all persons or related to earnings? The wage-related principle in social insurance seems to be gaining ground throughout the world. The provision of differential benefits related to wages has several objectives: preserving the worker's motivation for making the maximum contribution to the economy, relating benefits to diverse economic situations, and relating benefits to different standards of living.

Many questions arise as to the financing of social security programs. Should workers and/or employers contribute directly to the program through earmarked payroll taxes? Or should the system be financed from general taxes? In the United States, our social insurance programs are contributory; our assistance programs are financed from general taxes. In some countries where the contributory principle is dominant, the government also contributes to the social insurance system. At present, there appears little likelihood that there will be government contributions to our social insurance programs on any extensive scale. The distribution of the cost likewise raises many questions. Who should bear the cost and how much should each party bear? In California's temporary disability program, the worker bears all of the cost; in workmen's compensation in virtually all states, the employer bears all of the cost; in unemployment insurance, the employer bears the cost (with some minor exceptions); in old-age, survivors, and disability insurance, the cost is shared equally by employer and employee. In public assistance, the benefits are paid from general taxes. How much should be paid (in public assistance) by the Federal Government, and how much by the states and/or localities?

Other issues also are under current discussion. Should there be trust funds in the social insurance programs? Should the trust funds be invested in government securities? Is the financing actuarially sound? Should social insurance be put on a "pay as you go" basis? How should needed improvements in the various social insurance programs be financed? Should the tax rate in old-age, survivors, and disability insurance be allowed to rise while the maximum taxable earnings limit remains the same? Should public assistance be financed out of general funds or earmarked taxes?

Students of public administration are raising questions about the administrative aspects of our social security programs. Must the present complex administrative arrangements continue? Can they be simplified? Old-age, survivors, and disability insurance is a Federally administered program, but disability determinations under this program are made by state agencies; the states operate unemployment insurance under Federal law but without much Federal supervision or Federal standards; workmen's compensation is entirely a state program with some states having state insurance funds and others having workmen's compensation insurance primarily with private carriers; the public assistance categories are state programs with Federal grants-in-aid; general assistance is entirely a state program in some states, a local program in others, a joint state and local program in others.

In seeking to protect the American people from the risk of stoppage of income, questions will continue to be debated as to what additional risks shall be covered. Should a family allowance system be established? At present, there is considerable agitation for medical care coverage for the aged, but very little effective interest in family allowances.

Finally, a number of fundamental and basic questions must continue to occupy our attention. How much economic security can a society afford? How much is the individual willing to reduce his take-home pay in order to insure against the risks of economic insecurity? In some countries the total social security taxes exceed 40 per cent of payroll. How much of the nation's income should be devoted to social security programs? These are broad economic, social, and political problems which increasingly will demand the attention of social security policy makers.

The questions and issues are legion—those mentioned above represent only a few of the more important ones. The answers will shape and improve America's social security system in the years to come. For surely it will be improved. The growth of the United States social security program has been faster than that of the program of any other large industrial country in the past twenty-five years. In spite of differences of opinion as to various aspects of social security and related programs, the United States is committed to making economic security a reality in the lives of all Americans. In achieving this goal, social security programs play a fundamental and significant role.

Footnotes and Tables

Footnotes

1. W. L. MacKenzie King, Canadian Prime Minister, Toronto, October 9, 1942.
2. U. S. Social Security Board, *First Annual Report,* Fiscal Year Ending June 30, 1936, Foreword, p. v. Washington: U. S. Government Printing Office, 1937.
3. United States Social Security Act, 49 Stat. 620
4. International Labor Office, *Social Security, A Worker's Education Manual.* Geneva, 1958, p. 12.
5. U. S. Bureau of Old-Age and Survivors Insurance, *Your Social Security: Old-Age, Survivors and Disability Insurance Benefits Under the Social Security Law.* (OASI-35) Washington: U. S. Government Printing Office, 1960.
6. *Helvering v. Davis,* 301 United States 619, 641, 57 Sup. Ct. 904, 908, 81 L. Ed. 1307 (1937). (The Supreme Court decision declaring the old-age benefits portion of the Social Security Act constitutional.)
7. U. S. Social Security Administration, *Research and Statistics Note 30— 1960.* p. 8. (Mimeographed.)
8. H. M. Somers and A. R. Somers, *Workmen's Compensation.* New York: John Wiley & Sons, Inc., 1954, p. 2.
9. U. S. National Health Survey, *Disability Days Due to Injury.* Washington: U. S. Department of Health, Education, and Welfare, Public Health Service, 1963. (Health Statistics, ser. B-40) p. 1.
10. International Labor Office, *op. cit.,* pp. 2-7.
11. *Ibid.,* p. 3.
12. *Ibid.,* pp. 3-4.
13. G. F. McCleary, *National Health Insurance.* London: H. K. Lewis & Co., Ltd., 1932, p. 9.
14. *Ibid.,* p. 19.
15. Daniel Defoe, *An Essay Upon Projects: A Pension Office.* 1698.
16. McCleary, *op. cit.,* p. 21.
17. Maxwell S. Stewart, *Social Security.* New York: W. W. Norton & Co., 1939, p. 123.
18. U. S. Committee on Economic Security, *Social Security in America: The Factual Background of the Social Security Act as Summarized from Staff Reports to the Committee . . . Published for the Committee . . . by the Social Security Board.* Washington: U. S. Government Printing Office, 1937, p. 470.
19. Stewart, *op. cit.,* p. 126.
20. International Labor Office, *op. cit.,* p. 10.
21. Max Lerner, *America as a Civilization.* New York: Simon and Schuster, 1957, p. 131.
22. 26 Stat. 1097.
23. William E. Smythe, "A New Homestead Policy for America," *Review of Reviews,* March 1922, pp. 291-296.
24. *Franklin v. United Railways and Electric Workers of Baltimore,* 2 Baltimore City Reports 309 (1904).
25. Abraham Epstein, *Insecurity: A Challenge to America.* New York: Random House, 2nd rev. ed. 1938, p. 591.

26. Somers and Somers, *op. cit.*, p. 31.

27. *State Board of Control v. Buckstage*, 18 Ariz. 277, 158 P. 837 (1916).

28. Barbara N. Armstrong, *Insuring The Essentials*. New York: The Macmillan Co., 1932, p. 434.

29. *Ibid.*, p. 436.

30. Dr. Rubinow was Chief Statistician of the Ocean Accident and Guarantee Corporation and President of the Casualty Actuarial Society, 1914–1916.

31. I. M. Rubinow, *Social Insurance*. New York: Henry Holt and Co., 1913, p. iii.

32. Armstrong, *op. cit.*

33. Epstein, *op. cit.*

34. Francis E. Townsend, *New Horizons (An Autobiography)*, Jesse George Murray, ed. Chicago: J. L. Stewart, 1943, p. 138.

35. U. S. President (Franklin D. Roosevelt), Fireside Chat, September 30, 1934.

36. Arthur M. Schlesinger, Jr., *The Crisis of the Old Order: 1919–1933*. Boston: Houghton Mifflin Co., 1957, p. 155.

37. *Ibid.*, p. 155.

38. *Ibid.*, p. 159.

39. United States Bureau of Labor Statistics, *Monthly Labor Review*, March 1931, pp. 48–55.

40. Schlesinger, *op. cit.*, p. 178.

41. Pennsylvania, R.I., Wisc., Ill., Ohio, N.Y., N.J.

42. Samuel E. Bennett, *Unemployment and Relief from the Local Government Point of View*. Chicago: Public Administration Service, 1955, p. 28.

43. *Ibid.*, p. 37.

44. Edwin E. Witte, "Twenty Years of Social Security," *Social Security Bulletin*, October 1955, p. 19.

45. Executive Order No. 6757, June 29, 1934, quoted in U.S. Committee on Economic Security, *Social Security in America*, p. iii.

46. Secretary of Labor, Frances Perkins; Secretary of the Treasury, Henry Morgenthau, Jr.; Attorney General, Homer Cummings; Secretary of Agriculture, Henry Wallace; Federal Emergency Relief Administrator, Harry Hopkins.

47. The advisory committees were: actuarial, medical, public health, hospital, dental, public employment and public assistance, child welfare, and nursing.

48. Edwin E. Witte, "Birth and Early Days of Social Security in the United States," *Public Welfare*, July 1960, p. 141.

49. *Ibid.*, pp. 141–142.

50. U. S. President (Franklin D. Roosevelt), *Report of the Committee on Economic Security, Message from the President*. (74th Congress, 1st Session, House. Doc. 81) Washington: U. S. Government Printing Office, 1935.

51. U. S. Committee on Economic Security, *Report to the President*. Washington: U. S. Government Printing Office, 1935, pp. 29–34.

52. *Ibid.*, pp. 34–35.

53. *Ibid.*, pp. 25–29.

54. *Ibid.*, pp. 10–23.

55a. and 55b. *Ibid.*, pp. 35–41.

56. S. 1130, 74th Congress, 1st session 1935.

57. H. R. 4120, 74th Congress, 1st session 1935.

58. Hearings before Committee on Finance on S. 1130, 74th Congress, 1st session 1935.

59. Hearings before Committee on Ways and Means on H. R. 4120, 74th Congress, 1st session 1935.

60. Witte, "Birth and Early Days of Social Security in the United States," *op. cit.*, p. 142.

61. 49 Stat. 620.

62. Arthur M. Schlesinger, Jr., *The Coming of the New Deal.* Boston: Houghton Mifflin Co., 1959, p. 312.

63. U. S. Committee on Economic Security, *Report to the President,* pp. 41–43.

64. Title II, Social Security Act of 1935.

65. Title I, Social Security Act of 1935.

66. Title III, VII, IX, Social Security Act of 1935.

67. Title IV, Social Security of 1935.

68. Title V, Social Security Act of 1935.

69. Title X, Social Security Act of 1935.

70. 1939–53 Stat. 1360 (1939).
1946–60 Stat. 978 (1946).
1950–64 Stat. 477 (1950).
1952–66 Stat. 767 (1952)
1954–68 Stat. 1052 (1954).
1956–70 Stat. 807 (1956).
1958–72 Stat. 938, 964, 1013, 1778 (1958).
1960–74 Stat. 924, 81 (1960).
1961–75 Stat. 8, 31, 75 (1961).
1962–Public Welfare Amendments of 1962 (H. R. 10606), 76 Stat. 172 (1962).

71. *Steward Machine Co. v. Davis,* 301 United States 548, 57 Sup. Ct. 883, 81 L. Ed. 1279 (1937).

72. *Helvering v. Davis,* 301 United States 619, 57 Sup. Ct. 904, 81 L. Ed. 1307 (1937).

73. Arthur M. Schlesinger, Jr., *The Coming of the New Deal,* p. 315.

74. *Ibid.*

75. *Ewing v. Gardner,* 185 F. 2d 781, 784 (1950).

76. *Ekus v. Altmeyer,* 52 F. Suppl. 306 (E.D.N.Y. 1943).

77. Persons interested in a more complete and detailed discussion may obtain the *Social Security Handbook on Old-Age, Survivors, and Disability Insurance:* Social Security Administration, U.S. Department of Health, Education, and Welfare, Washington: U.S. Government Printing Office, 1960. Attorneys will find a useful volume published by the American Law Institute: Charles I. Schottland and Ewell T. Bartlett, *Federal Social Security, a Guide to Law and Procedure,* Joint Committee on Continuing Legal Education of the American Law Institute and the American Bar Association, Philadelphia, 1959.

78. J. Douglas Brown, "The American Philosophy of Social Insurance," *The Social Service Review,* March 1956, p. 6.

79. Stefan A. Riesenfeld, "The Place of Unemployment Insurance Within the Patterns and Policies of Protection Against Wage Loss," *Vanderbilt Law Review,* February 1955, p. 218.

80. *Report of the Committee on the Economic and Financial Problems of the Provision for Old Age,* cmd. No. 9333, Sec. 167 (1954). Great Britain.

81. U. S. Advisory Council on Social Security Financing, *Financing Old-Age, Survivors, and Disability Insurance.* Washington: U. S. Government Printing Office, 1959, Sec. V, p. 3.

82. U. S. Advisory Council on Social Security Financing, *op. cit.;* Senate Committee on Finance, *Digest of Issues in Social Security,* 80th Congress, 1st session (1947); Senate Committee on Finance, *A Report From the Advisory Council on Social Security,* S. Doc. 204, 80th Congress, 2nd session (1948).

83. J. Douglas Brown, "The American Philosophy of Social Insurance," *The Social Service Review,* March 1956, p. 4.

84. For a discussion of the history, background, and controversies around the retirement test, see Wilbur J. Cohen, *Retirement Policies Under Social Security,* Berkeley: University of California Press, 1957, pp. 69–95; and *The Retirement Test Under Old-Age and Survivors Insurance,* A Report Submitted

to the Committee on Ways and Means of the House of Representatives by the Department of Health, Education, and Welfare. Washington: U. S. Government Printing Office, 1960.

85. U. S. Laws, *Compilation of the Social Security Laws* . . . Washington: U. S. Government Printing Office, 1961.

86. Title XX, Federal Regulations and Cumulative Supplements, 1949 ed. Washington: U. S. Government Printing Office, 1949.

87. A good discussion of the various issues and unfinished tasks will be found in Eveline M. Burns, *Social Security and Public Policy*. New York: McGraw-Hill Book Co., 1956.

88. J. Henry Richardson, *Economic and Financial Aspects of Social Security*. Toronto: University of Toronto Press, 1960, p. 9.

89. U. S. Social Security Administration, Division of Program Research, *Social Security Programs Throughout the World, 1961*. Washington: U. S. Government Printing Office, 1961.

90. Gordon Wagenet, "Twenty-Five Years of Unemployment Insurance in the United States," *Social Security Bulletin*, August 1960, p. 50.

91. Under "temporary" legislation enacted in 1961, the rate is raised to 3.5 per cent for 1962–63 and the additional tax income to the Federal Government is used to finance a temporary "extended unemployment benefits" provision.

92. William Haber and Wilbur J. Cohen, *Social Security—Programs, Problems, and Policies*. Selected Readings. Homewood, Ill.: Richard D. Irwin, Inc., 1960, p. 253.

93. *Ibid.*, p. 254.

94. U. S. President (Franklin D. Roosevelt), Second Inaugural Address, January 20, 1937.

95. Title I, Social Security Act as Amended.

96. Title IV.

97. Title X.

98. Title XIV.

99. Alaska, Arizona, Indiana, and Nevada.

100. White House Conference, 1909, *Proceedings of the Conference on the Care of Dependent Children*, held at Washington, D.C., January 1909. Washington: U. S. Government Printing Office, 1909, pp. 9–10.

101. State plans are set out in detail in *Characteristics of State Public Assistance Plans*, Bureau of Family Services, Social Security Administration, United States Department of Health, Education, and Welfare, Public Assistance Report No. 49. Washington: U. S. Government Printing Office, 1962.

102. 64 Stat. 549.

103. Alaska, Arizona, Indiana, and Nevada.

104. 75 Stat. 75.

105. Message of President Kennedy to Congress, Feb. 1, 1962.

106. See *Characteristics of General Assistance in the United States*. Prepared by the Bureau of Public Assistance, Social Security Administration, U. S. Department of Health, Education, and Welfare. Washington: U. S. Government Printing Office, 1959.

107. President Theodore Roosevelt, 1907.

108. Epstein, *op. cit.*, p. 584.

109. Somers and Somers, *op. cit.*, p. 29.

110. Stewart, *op. cit.*, p. 70.

111. Rubinow, *op. cit.*, p. 159.

112. Edwin E. Witte, "The Theory of Workmen's Compensation," *American Labor Legislation Review*, December 1930. In the case of *Nagy v. Ford Motor Co.*, 78 Atl. 2d 709 (1951), the court made it clear that the workmen's compensation act "provides social insurance in the common interest as well as the interest of the injured workman," p. 713.

113. For the most comprehensive current critical study of workmen's compensation, see Somers and Somers, *Workmen's Compensation.*

114. H. M. Somers, "Myth and Reality in Workmen's Compensation." In Haber and Cohen, *op. cit.*, p. 435.

115. Sir William Beveridge, *Social Insurance and Allied Services.* New York: The Macmillan Co., 1942, pp. 35–46.

116. Some have features of both, depending on the particular industry. See *Analysis of Workmen's Compensation Laws.* Washington, D.C.: Chamber of Commerce of the United States, 1960, Chart XIII, pp. 54–55.

117. Alfred M. Skolnik, "New Benchmarks in Workmen's Compensation," *Social Security Bulletin,* June 1962, p. 6.

118. Generalizations such as this are difficult to make. Some compulsory laws cover only hazardous industries and there are numerous exceptions.

119. Somers and Somers, *op. cit.*, p. 59.

120. Oregon requires one cent a day from employees, and some states require employee contributions toward medical payment.

121. Somers and Somers, *op. cit.*, p. 144.

122. Philip Guedalla, *The Hundredth Year.* New York: Doubleday, Doran Co., 1939.

123. U. S. Social Security Administration, *Social Security in the United States.* Washington: U. S. Government Printing Office, 1959, p. 35.

124. 48 Stat. 1283.

125. *Railroad Retirement Board et al. v. Alton Railroad Co. et al.*, 295 United States 330, 55 Sup. Ct. 758 (1935).

126. The tax was on a maximum of $300 per month prior to July 1954, $350 per month from July 1954 through May 1959, and $400 a month since June 1959.

127. Henry Clay. Speech at Lexington, Kentucky, May 16, 1829.

128. Dorrance C. Bronson, *Concepts of Actuarial Soundness in Pension Plans.* Homewood, Ill.: Richard D. Irwin, Inc., 1957, p. 6.

129. Samuel Johnson. In James Boswell, *Life of Johnson,* ed. George Birkbeck Hill. Oxford: Clarendon Press, 1887, Vol. IV, p. 362.

130. Grant M. Osborn, *Compulsory Temporary Disability Insurance in the United States.* Homewood, Ill.: Richard D. Irwin, Inc., 1958, p. 16.

131. Sickness Insurance Acts: Germany 1883, Austria 1888, Hungary 1891, Luxembourg 1901, Norway 1909, Great Britain 1911, Rumania 1912, Russia 1912.

132. U. S. Social Security Administration, *Research and Statistics Note 17 —1960.* (Mimeographed.)

133. Alfred M. Skolnik, "Income Loss Protection Against Short-Term Sickness, 1948–1960," *Social Security Bulletin,* January 1962, p. 3.

134. U. S. Bureau of Employment Security, *Significant Temporary Disability Insurance Data, 1959.* (BES sub series) Washington: The Bureau, 1961.

135. Shakespeare, *Hamlet.*

136. Veterans Affairs, *Annual Report 1960.* Washington: U. S. Government Printing Office, 1961, p. 1.

137. Journals of Congress, i, 454–458.

138. United States Statutes at Large, 1 Stat. 95.

139. (Korean Conflict veterans) 72 Stat. 1176.
(World War II veterans) 58 Stat. 284.

140. 73 Stat. 432.

141. Veterans Affairs, *Annual Report 1960,* p. 58.

142. 58 Stat. 291 was extended to February 1, 1975, by 75 Stat. 201.

143. Benjamin Franklin.

144. For an extensive review of the history of industrial pensions, see Murray W. Latimer, *Industrial Pension Systems in the United States and Canada.* New York: Industrial Relations Counselors, Inc., 1932.

145. U. S. Steel Industry Board, *Report to the President of the United States on the Labor Dispute in the Basic Steel Industry . . . Submitted September 10, 1949.* Washington: U. S. Government Printing Office, 1949, p. 55.

146. Albert de Roots, "Pensions as Wages," *The American Economic Review,* June 1913, p. 287.

147. Alfred M. Skolnik, "Trends in Employee Benefit Plans, 1954–59: Part II," *Social Security Bulletin,* May 11, 1961, p. 13.

148. New Testament, I Timothy, vi, 19.

149. *Life Insurance Fact Book, 1960.* New York: Institute of Life Insurance, 1960, p. 5. The figures and statistics in this section on life insurance are taken from the above source.

150. United States Savings and Loan League, *Savings and Loan Fact Book '61.* Chicago, 1961, p. 9.

151. *Ibid.,* pp. 70, 71.

152. Arthur J. Altmeyer, first United States Commissioner for Social Security, September 1945.

153. The important issues have been well presented in Eveline M. Burns, *op. cit.;* and in William Haber and Wilbur J. Cohen, *Readings in Social Security.* New York: Prentice-Hall, Inc., 1948.

154. Arthur M. Altmeyer, "Ten Years of Social Security," *Survey Graphic,* Vol. XXXIV, September 1945, p. 369.

155. Robert M. Ball, *Social Security's Role in the Economic Future of Older People.* Speech given by Mr. Ball, present Commissioner of Social Security, at Annual Meeting of the National Council on the Aging, October 9, 1961, New York, 1961. (Mimeographed.)

Table I
OASDI Benefits Related to Insured Status [a]

Benefits are payable to:	If the worker is:
1. A retired worker age 62 or over.	Fully insured.
2. A disabled worker.	Fully insured and disability insured, i.e., has 20 quarters of coverage out of the 40 quarters ending when he is disabled.
3. A wife of a worker entitled to retirement or disability benefits if she is age 62 or over or is caring for a child entitled to benefits.	Entitled to old-age or disability benefits.
4. A dependent, unmarried child of a worker entitled to old-age or disability benefits if the child is under 18 or has a disability which began before the child was 18.	Entitled to old-age or disability benefits.
5. A dependent husband, age 62 or over, of a worker entitled to old-age or disability benefits.	Entitled to old-age or disability benefits and is currently insured.
6. A widow, age 62 or over, of a deceased worker.	Fully insured.
7. A widow or former divorced wife of deceased worker who is caring for his child entitled to benefits.	Either fully or currently insured.
8. A dependent, unmarried child of a deceased worker if the child is under 18 or under a disability which began before the child was 18.	Either fully or currently insured.
9. Dependent widower, age 62 or over, of a deceased worker.	Both fully and currently insured.
10. Dependent parents, age 62 or over, of a deceased worker.	Fully insured.
A lump-sum death payment may be made to the widow or widower living with the worker at his death; (or to the person who paid the funeral expenses) if there is no eligible spouse, to the funeral home for unpaid expenses, or, if paid, to the person who paid them.	Either fully or currently insured.

[a] *Social Security Handbook on Old-Age, Survivors, and Disability Insurance.* Department of Health, Education and Welfare, Washington, D.C.: U. S. Government Printing Office, 1960, p. 23.

Table II

Examples of OASDI Monthly Payments

	Average Yearly Earnings after 1950		
	$ 3,000	$ 4,200	$ 4,800
Retirement at 62	$ 76.00	$ 92.80	$101.60
Retirement at 63	82.40	100.60	110.10
Retirement at 64	88.70	108.30	118.60
Retirement at 65 or over	95.00	116.00	127.00
Wife's benefit at 62	35.70	43.50	47.70
Wife's benefit at 63	39.60	48.40	53.00
Wife's benefit at 64	43.60	53.20	58.30
Wife's benefit at 65 or with child in her care	47.50	58.00	63.50
Widow 62 or over	78.40	95.70	104.80
Widow under 62 and 1 child	142.60	174.00	190.60
Widow under 62 and 2 children	202.40	254.00	254.00
One surviving child	71.30	87.00	95.30
Two surviving children	142.60	174.00	180.60
Maximum for one family	202.40	254.00	254.00
Lump-sum death payment	255.00	255.00	255.00

Table III

Application of the Yearly Portion of the OASDI Retirement Test for Illustrative Amounts of Annual Earnings

Annual Earnings	Amount of Benefits Withheld in Year*
$1,200 or less	None
1,300	$ 50
1,400	100
1,500	150
1,600	200
1,700	250
1,800	350
1,900	450
2,000	550
2,400	950
2,800	1,350
3,200	1,750
3,600	2,150
4,000	2,550
4,400**	2,950

* For retired workers, withholding is made against the total family benefits. For dependent and survivor beneficiaries with earnings, the withholding is only made against their own benefits. Obviously, the withholding (as shown in this table) cannot exceed the total benefits otherwise payable.

** For earnings of $4,498 or more, under no circumstances will any benefits be payable according to the yearly test.

Note: If the application of the monthly portion of the retirement test is advantageous, the amount of benefits withheld will be less than shown above (see text).

Table IV

Government Employees Covered by Retirement Systems, December 1961
(In thousands of persons)

Category	Number Employed	Number Covered by a Public Retirement System	Percentage Covered by a Public Retirement System [a]	Number Under OASDI Only	Number Under Both OASDI and another Retirement System
Federal Civil Service Retirement	2,060	2,060	100	——	——
Armed Forces	2,810	2,810	100	——	2,810
Other Federal	170	170	100	150	15
State and Local	6,470	5,820	90	1,100	2,600
Total	11,510	10,860	94	1,250	5,425

[a] Including old-age, survivors, and disability insurance.

Table V

Monthly Beneficiaries Under Public Employee Retirement System—
June 30, 1961 [a] (In thousands)

Retirement System	Total	Age and Service	Disability	Survivor
Grand Total	1,572.3	1,072.3	266.9	233.1
Total Federal	869.3	497.3	204.9	167.1
Civil Service Retirement	559.1	284.3	112.2	162.6
Other Contributory	5.0	4.0	.4	.6
Armed Forces	292.6	202.0	87.8	2.8
Other Noncontributory	12.6	7.0	4.4	1.1
Total State and Local	703.0	575.0	62.0	66.0

[a] Research and Statistics Note No. 11—1962, May 16, 1962. Department of Health, Education, and Welfare, Social Security Administration, Division of Program Research.

Table VI

Total Benefit Payments Under Public Employee Retirement Systems, 1961 [a]
(In millions)

Retirement System	Total	Age and Service	Disability	Survivor Monthly	Lump-sum
Grand Total	$3,014.8	$2,191.4	$535.2	$203.3	$84.9
Total Federal	1,804.8	1,241.4	425.2	123.3	14.9
Civil Service Retirement	908.7	604.5	172.8	117.7	13.7
Other Contributory	13.2	10.3	.6	1.2	1.1
Armed Forces	845.3	602.5	239.6	3.2	——
Other Noncontributory	37.6	24.2	12.2	1.2	——
Total State and Local	1,210.0	950.0	110.0	80.0	70.0

[a] Research and Statistics Note No. 11—1962, May 16, 1962. Department of Health, Education, and Welfare, Social Security Administration, Division of Program Research.

Table VII

Proportion of State and Local Government Employees
with Specified Retirement Coverage—January 1961

Retirement Coverage	State Government (1,600,000 employees)	County Government (700,000 employees)	Local Government (4,000,000 employees)	Total (6,300,000 employees)
OASDI and other plan	55%	41%	36%	41%
OASDI	13	36	17	19
Other plan only	19	12	35	28
No plan	13	11	12	12
Total	100	100	100	100

Table VIII

Hospitalization Insurance, Estimated Enrollment,
and Rate Per Thousand

Year	Total [*]	Group Insurance Policies	Individual Insurance Policies	Blue Cross Plans	Other Plans
1959	127,896,000	51,255,000	31,718,000	53,649,000	8,038,000
1949	66,044,000	17,697,000	14,729,000	33,381,000	4,694,000
		Rate Per Thousand Population			
1959	725	291	180	304	46
1949	448	120	100	226	32

[*] Unduplicated total number of different persons with any of these types of protection.

Table IX

Estimated Number of Workers and Dependents Covered under Employee
Benefit Plans, by Type of Benefit, December 31, 1960 [a]

Type of Benefit	Number Covered (in millions)
All workers and their dependents:	
Life insurance and death benefits	46.5
Accidental death and dismemberment	20.9
Hospitalization	103.5
Surgical	98.8
Regular medical	74.8
Major medical expense	25.6
Workers in private industry:	
Temporary disability	25.5
Supplemental unemployment benefits	1.7
Retirement	21.6

[a] Skolnik, Alfred M, "Employee Benefit Plans, 1954-60," *Social Security Bulletin*, April 1962, p. 7.

INDEX